In All Your Ways

In All Your Ways

A Study of Proverbs

Andrew W. Blackwood, Jr.

BAKER BOOK HOUSE
Grand Rapids, Michigan

Acknowledgments

The following publishers have graciously extended permission to use copyrighted materials:

Doubleday and Company, New York, for quotations from *The Jerusalem Bible*, © 1966 by Darton, Longman & Todd , Ltd., and Doubleday and Company, Inc.; from R. B. Y. Scott, *Proverbs, Ecclesiastes; The Anchor Bible*, © 1965 by Doubleday and Company, Inc.

Harcourt Brace Jovanovich, Inc., New York, for quotations from C. S. Lewis, *Reflections on the Psalms*.

Harper & Row, Publishers, Inc., New York, for quotations from James Moffatt, *The Bible, A New Translation*, © 1922, 1924, 1926, 1935 by Harper & Bros.

The Delegates of the Oxford University Press and the Syndics of the Cambridge University Press, New York, for quotations from *The New English Bible*, © 1961, 1970.

Thomas Nelson, Inc., Nashville, Tennessee, for quotations from the *New American Bible*, © 1970 by the Confraternity of Christian Doctrine, Washington, D.C., and used by permission of the copyright owner. All rights reserved.

Tyndale House Publishers, Wheaton, Illinois, for quotations from *The Living Bible*, © 1971.

The University of Chicago Press, for quotations from Edgar J. Goodspeed, *The Apocrypha: An American Translation*, © 1938 by Edgar J. Goodspeed. All rights reserved.

Abbreviations

AJV   *The American Jewish Version*, published in 1917 by the Jewish Publishing Society of America.

Goodspeed   *The Apocrypha: An American Translation*, by Edgar J. Goodspeed. Composed and published in 1938 by the University of Chicago Press.

JB   *The Jerusalem Bible.* All quotations are from the Standard Edition, published in 1966.

KJV   *The King James* (or Authorized) *Version*, the incomparable translation of the Bible, published in 1611.

Moffatt   *The Bible, A New Translation*, by James Moffatt, first published in 1922.

NAB   The *New American Bible*, © 1970 by the Confraternity of Christian Doctrine.

R. B. Y. Scott   *Proverbs, Ecclesiastes; The Anchor Bible*, © 1965 by Doubleday and Company, Inc.

RSV   *The Revised Standard Version*, © 1971, 1973, by the Division of Christian Education of the National Council of the Churches of Christ in the U.S.A.

TLB   *The Living Bible*, published in 1971 by Tyndale House Publishers.

To

Our grandchildren

With more love than you will
believe possible, until you are
grandparents.

A Few Words of Gratitude

I am grateful to the professor in seminary who said, "When you don't know what to preach about next Sunday, fall back on Proverbs." During my first years in the pastorate I applied the advice freely and fell in love with the book. Other enthusiasms have waned, but this one has grown steadily. I thank the good Lord for including Proverbs in the Bible. Like my distinguished predecessor Peter, I must say of many biblical writings that I find "some things in them hard to understand" (II Peter 3:16). But Proverbs is crystal clear, most of the time, a ready help to a young preacher in need.

I am grateful to the congregations in Newton, Columbus, West Palm Beach, and Atlanta with whom I have been privileged to share my love for Proverbs. They have joined me in laughing at the funny ones and wincing when a barb hit a tender spot. Practically everything that follows began as sermons, preached to Christians whose love has sustained me.

I am grateful to my wife, Mary Ann, for constant encouragement and practical suggestions, for pointing out infelicities of thought and expression, and for discovering answers where all I could find were questions. I am grateful to her for living what the concluding poem in Proverbs is all about.

I am grateful to four other women who have shared in the

preparation and criticism of the manuscript. Helen Austin, Betty MacCormack, Margaret Morris, and Marion Steele have contributed far more than technical skill, of which they have a great deal. With charitable candor they have pointed out my divergences from English usage. My creative spelling and my free-wheeling punctuation have, alas, been subdued. Flights of illogic were grounded. I am grateful for their help; I am grateful for their friendship.

I am grateful to my long-time friend, Professor Alexander Christie, recently retired as teacher of Old Testament at Union Theological Seminary Philippines, Philippine Islands. Dr. Christie is much like the wise people of ancient Israel, combining inflexible penetration to the heart of an issue with gentle, puckish humor. From the inception of the work, we have discussed the many problems of organization and interpretation that necessarily arise in every biblical study. I appreciate his many kindly criticisms. I hereby exonerate him, and the others mentioned above, from all culpability for my remaining shortcomings.

I am grateful to the many other scholars whose work has helped me through the rough places. A book of this nature does not call for a forest of footnotes nor a voluminous bibliography. Let it suffice that I have received most of my help from three writers: first, my beloved professor, Charles T. Fritsch, writing for *The Interpreter's Bible*; second, Dr. A. Cohen for his commentary in *The Soncino Books of the Bible*, which gives valuable insights into Talmudic, medieval, and contemporary Jewish scholarship; and third, R. B. Y. Scott, who translated and commented on Proverbs for *The Anchor Bible*. My indebtedness to him will be readily apparent to the reader. Were I addicted to consistency, I would have identified the quotations from his work as *Anchor Bible*, rather than by name of translator. The editors of the *Anchor Bible* are outstanding scholars, but they didn't make the translation, Dr. Scott did.

I am grateful to the other translators, most of whose names are unknown to me, who have labored to produce The Jerusalem Bible, The New English Bible, The New American Bible, and the other excellent translations that have appeared during our turbulent twentieth century. For beauty, no contemporary translation approaches the beloved King James Version, but the Bible is supposed to reach the head as well as the heart, and the English language has marched from its standing place in 1611. So I have based this essay on The Revised Standard Version, and drawn freely upon others to illustrate different aspects of a thought and occasional downright contradictions. Of the contradictions, Dr. Scott muses plaintively that the reader "may wonder how they can differ as much as they do since all (presumably) are translations of the same original text." I have mentioned a few of the technical problems, when it seemed germane to do so, and have tried to show why excellent scholars may reach different conclusions.

But chiefly I am grateful to the divine love that is communicated to us in many ways. He spoke with thunder on Mount Sinai. His prophets caught the bolts of lightning and in God's name they thundered, "Thus saith the Lord!" We Protestants tend to undervalue the work of the priests who kept the machinery of faith operating through long centuries of darkness. God likewise spoke—and speaks—through the voices of those striving to be wise. And the heart of his teaching is:

> In all your ways acknowledge him,
> and he will make straight your paths   (Prov. 3:6).

Andrew W. Blackwood, Jr.

Contents

1

God's Book of Family Life

The following essay concerns your using an important part of the Bible for its intended purpose—to help you and your family in the daily walk with God. Proverbs consists of brief meditations, most of them only a sentence in length, that have helped countless others on the journey.

Solitary meditation has always been an integral part of Christianity (Ps. 1:2). When Christians fail to emphasize this part of our faith, we should not be surprised if the Eastern religions rush in to fill the gap resulting from our adherence to the cult of Martha while ignoring the good example of Mary (Luke 10:38–42). We all would be better Christians if we made a daily practice of thinking, alone, about our faith. The Book of Proverbs is a God-given aid to meditation. Here important thoughts are expressed concisely, often beautifully, in an easily remembered form. If meditation has not been your habit, don't start off with a great chunk of time; you will find it difficult enough to concentrate on one subject for three minutes. So start with three minutes. Then, as your skill and schedule permit, increase the time devoted to what well may become the most important part of your entire day.

No law, of which I am aware, requires Christians today to forsake our grandparents' wise practice of conducting daily family worship. The patterns varied widely, but a typical family devotion would include a brief reading from the Scripture, a short prayer spoken by the mother or father, and the entire family uniting in the Lord's Prayer. When you read about the practice of family worship in Victorian novels you discover why many have discontinued it; all too often our ancestors forgot about brevity, deciding that Jesus really meant somebody else (Matt. 6:7–8). If our forebears erred in praying overlong it is no improvement when we pray too little. Wherever Christian families gather to pray, Proverbs is in frequent use. I am writing with the hope and prayer that your family will come to know and to love this book, which was included in the Holy Bible for folks just like you.

Proverbs is a book for the family. To be sure it contains wise counsel for the king, the soldier, the merchants, the banker, the courtier, and a lot of other important people, but most of its salty wisdom is directed to the family. Here you find relatively little about affairs of state, as in the prophetic writings, and few of the refulgent theological glories and perplexities that fill the rest of our Bible. Instead, you find page after page of practical, down-to-earth principles of daily life that have been tested and proved to be gold.

Since the Bible deals with the deepest of all matters, the relationship between God and humanity, you would expect to encounter many difficulties in its pages. But Proverbs is easy to read; the difficulty is living what you read. Parts of the Bible require much background in history and social customs, not Proverbs. Most of this book might have been written yesterday by a wise friend living just around the corner. Most of its message is immediately available to the modern mind, which badly needs some good news. Proverbs is packed with good news that psychologists keep rediscovering. You don't find all the wonder and mystery of Christian faith in Proverbs, but the sage counsel of this book will help you immeasurably in being a Christian.

You can read Proverbs and benefit without knowing when the book was written, or by whom. The basic principles of life are here to stay; their expression transcends all differences of culture. The wisdom extolled in Proverbs applies in Dubuque or Sacramento just as much as it applied in ancient Samaria or

Bethlehem. Even so, the more you know about the writers, their methods, their times, and their purposes, the more appreciative you will be.

Proverbs is gloriously old-fashioned. It lays heavy stress on hard work, thrift, sobriety, chastity, discipline, and reverence, all of which are in considerable disrepute today. But Proverbs bubbles over with something that seems to be missing from the lives of those who scoff at the old-fashioned virtures; Proverbs is filled with hope, laughter, song, loyalty, and stability. The theme of the book is expressed in one succinct sentence:

> In all your ways acknowledge him,
>   and he will make straight your paths   (3:6).

Proverbs depicts the strong, constructive life of those who walk in God-directed paths, and conversely, the tragedy of those who follow the way that leads to destruction.

We have a few destructive tools that were not available to our forebears, such as firearms, narcotics, and motorcycles. But these tools do not destroy except when their use is guided by Folly, a young woman to whom Proverbs introduces you—with urgent warning. Proverbs encourages you to walk each day with the other young woman, Wisdom, who helps you to develop positive qualities of spirit and whose companionship leads you to the eternal light.

My dictionary calls a proverb, "a brief, epigrammatic saying that is a popular byword; an oft-repeated, pithy, and ingeniously turned maxim." The dictionary tells me elsewhere that an epigram is a bright or witty saying, often involving an apparent contradiction, and a maxim is a profound utterance. I opened Proverbs at random and saw:

> The sacrifice of the wicked is an abomination to the Lord,
>   but the prayer of the upright is his delight   (15:8).

That is brief, very much to the point, and unutterably profound. It involves an apparent contradiction. Here is Mr. X who offers a huge sacrifice: he puts a big stained-glass window in the church. He offers to God something of great material value, but witholds what God really wants, his heart. Mr. Y cannot afford an expensive sacrifice, but he offers God his heart in prayer. Long before the proverb was composed, rich and poor people of spiritual integrity knew the truth it expresses. An unknown wise person wrapped a truth of experience into a superb sentence; that made it an epigram and a maxim. Then people by the dozen and the hundred and the thousand repeated it and passed it on to their children; that made it a proverb.

The Hebrew word for proverb, *mashal,* is derived, probably, from a verb meaning "resemble, be similar to." Many of the proverbs hinge upon a resemblance.

> He who is slack in his work
>   is a brother to him who destroys   (18:9).

The close relationship between sloth and destruction has occurred to all overseers and grandparents; expressing the truth required a brilliant mind. Chapter 26 is especially rich in proverbs of resemblance. The word "like" occurs in ten of its twenty-eight verses, the thought in most of the others.

> Like a sparrow in its flitting, like a swallow in its flying,
>   a curse that is causeless does not alight   (26:2).

> He who sends a message by the hand of a fool
>   cuts off his own feet and drinks violence   (26:6).

The idea of resemblance sometimes lies on a deeper level. One gem speaks scathingly of a fictitious character:

> The sluggard says, "There is a lion in the road!
>   There is a lion in the streets!"   (26:13).

If, in fact, a lion is roaming about, you would be well advised not to leave the house. If there is not a lion in the street, and you invent one to keep from doing what you ought to do, Proverbs has a pithy epithet dedicated to you, "sluggard." The obvious target of the proverb is the ready maker of excuses. An exasperated but still loving ancestor, quoting the maxim to a recalcitrant child would scarcely need to say, "You are like a sluggard who. . . ."

The Hebrew proverb, like that in English, is not limited to the idea of resemblance. It may be a concise, simple statement of a profound truth.

Those who forsake the law praise the wicked
  but those who keep the law strive against them   (28:4).

If *mashal* originally meant "likeness," its meaning expanded. It includes the idea of a parable, to the extent that the Greek translation of the Old Testament, the Septuagint, uses the two terms interchangeably. The best example of a parable in Proverbs is The Sluggard's Vineyard:

I passed by the field of a sluggard,
  by the vineyard of a man without sense;
and lo, it was all overgrown with thorns;
  the ground was covered with nettles,
  and its stone wall was broken down.
Then I saw and considered it;
  I looked and received instruction.
"A little sleep, a little slumber,
  a little folding of the hands to rest,"
and poverty will come upon you like a robber,
  and want like an armed man   (24:30–34).

The principal difference between a proverb and a parable is length. A proverb is short and pithy. A parable, as Jesus has shown, may be an extended story with many characters. If it is a good parable, like The Sluggard's Vineyard or those of Jesus, the point is sharp.

Proverbs contains other ways of expressing thoughts. It begins with an extended essay on wisdom and concludes with a superb poem, The Courageous Woman, neither of which fits our idea of a proverb. But the Hebrew term has a genial flexibility that our English word lacks. Balaam's prophetic speech (Num. 23:7, etc.), is a *mashal*, as is Job's impassioned defense (Job 27:1, etc.), and the scholarly labor of the preacher (Eccles. 12:9). We could make quite a study of what *mashal* means in the Bible but our focus is upon the Book of Proverbs, most of which consists of what we call proverbs, and most of them speak to the constant questions of family life.

Proverbs, in English or Hebrew, usually fall into a few general patterns. You might find it interesting, as you read through the book, to classify each proverb. This mechanical labor will make you focus sharp attention on each verse of a book where the similarity in form of distantly related thoughts can lead you to drowsy skimming. The following list of seven general categories is adopted from R. B. Y. Scott, in *The Anchor Bible*. Dr. Scott says that neither this nor any other list of patterns is exhaustive.

1. Patterns of identity, equivalence, or invariable association:

A friend in need is a friend indeed.

Where there are no oxen, there is no grain;
   but abundant crops come by the strength of the ox   (14:4).

2. Patterns of contrast or paradox:

All that glitters is not gold.

He who is sated loathes honey,
   but to one who is hungry everything bitter is sweet   (27:7).

3. Patterns of similarity or type:

Time and tide wait for no man.

Like cold water to a thirsty soul,
   so is good news from a far country   (25:25).

4. Patterns of futility or absurdity; focus on what is contrary to right order:

Don't count your chickens before they are hatched.

As a door turns on its hinges,
   so does a sluggard on his bed   (26:14).

5. Patterns of classification and characterization:

A rolling stone gathers no moss.

A stone is heavy, and sand is weighty,
   but a fool's provocation is heavier than both   (27:3).

6. Patterns of value, priority, or proportion:

A bird in the hand is worth two in the bush.

What is desired in a man is loyalty,
   and a poor man is better than a liar   (19:22).

7. Patterns of behavior and the consequence of action:

Don't bite off more than you can chew.

He who digs a pit will fall into it,
   and a stone will come back upon him who starts it
      rolling   (26:27).

Most of the proverbs and other teachings that comprise the book are in poetry, employing the usual conventions of Hebrew poems in biblical time. The principal conventions in English poetry are rhyme and rhythm. As we all know, a jingle may have flawless rhyme and rhythm yet be a world apart from poetry; while the Gettysburg Address, though it has no pattern of rhyme or scansion, is a deathless poem. So you can have poetic conventions without poetry and poetry without poetic conventions.

Medieval and modern Hebrew poems use rhyme and rhythm much as we do in English, often with powerful effect. However, when rhyme occurs in a biblical poem, it usually appears to be accidental; systematic rhyme patterns are rare. The situation with rhythm differs, but not greatly. Great scholars in the early centuries of our faith reasoned that, since Greek and Latin poems have carefully worked-out rhythmic patterns, something similar must exist in biblical poems; so they sought eagerly for iambs and hexameters and the like, which simply are not there. The biblical writers did not use our poetic devices. They did, however, produce the world's greatest poetry.

Heroic efforts have been made to reproduce in English translation the rhythmic pattern of The Iliad or The Divine Comedy. Such an effort, when applied to the cadences of Hebrew poetry, is futile from the outset. Hebrew expressions are usually terse and condensed; Proverbs 15:27, for example, is nineteen words in English, only seven words in Hebrew. Obviously, the original cadence cannot be reflected in a translation, no matter how skilled the translator.

Other poetic devices, likewise difficult or impossible to translate, are assonance and alliteration. The former is the use of sharply contrasting sounds. The latter is using the same sound at the beginning of two or more words, as in "Sing a song of sixpence." When two languages differ as much in structure and vocabulary as do English and Hebrew, an attempt to translate such poetic conventions must represent the triumph of ingenuity over poetry.

The principal characteristic of Hebrew poetry, parallelism, can be translated. Look at the seven patterns of content suggested earlier, each illustrated with an English and a Hebrew proverb. You immediately notice that the English proverbs are all expressed in one line; the Hebrew in couplets. The two lines are "parallel," not with geometric rigor but with poetic beauty. Sometimes the thought of the first line is repeated in the second; sometimes the second line is in contrast to the first; and sometimes the two are related as cause and effect, or some other logical relationship. Sometimes, of course, the relationship between the two defies all attempts at classification.

In biblical studies today, the three chief types of parallelism are generally called synonymous, contrasted, and constructive parallelism.

1. *Synonymous Parallelism.* A statement is made, then made again in different words.

Pride goes before destruction,
    and a haughty spirit before a fall (16:18).

A worker's appetite works for him:
    his mouth urges him on (16:26).

A perverse man spreads strife,
　and a whisperer separates close friends　(16:28).

He who is slow to anger is better than the mighty,
　and he who rules his spirit than he who takes a city　(16:32).

2. *Contrasted Parallelism.* Here the truth expressed in the first clause is contrasted in the second. Often the proverb hinges upon the conjunction "and" (*w*), which is usually translated "but" when it introduces a contrast. All but one of the proverbs in chapter 13 are of this type.

A wise son hears his father's instruction,
　but a scoffer does not listen to rebuke　(13:1).

From the fruit of his mouth a good man eats good,
　but the desire of the treacherous is for violence　(13:2).

He who guards his mouth preserves his life;
　he who opens wide his lips comes to ruin　(13:3).

The soul of the sluggard craves, and gets nothing,
　while the soul of the diligent is richly supplied　(13:4).

The same conjunction occurs in verses 1, 2, and 4; there is no conjunction in verse 3; it is scarcely necessary.

3. *Constructive Parallelism.* Here are classified the many proverbs where the second clause develops the idea expressed in the first.

Leave the presence of a fool,
　for there you do not meet words of knowledge　(14:7).

The heart knows its own bitterness,
　and no stranger shares its joy　(14:10).

There is a way which seems right to a man,
　but its end is the way to death　(14:12).

In the fear of the Lord one has strong confidence,
　and his children will have a refuge　(14:26).

As you dig into Proverbs, you will find some groupings of verses with intricate parallel structure. For a simple example;

> Do not rob the poor because he is poor,
>   or crush the afflicted at the gate;
> for the Lord will plead their cause
>   and despoil of life those who despoil them   (22:22–23).

The first two lines are synonymous parallelism; one who takes legal advantage of the poor is equal to a thief. The second couplet forms a constructive parallel with the first couplet; it shows the effect of evil action. But within the second is another constructive parallel; pleading the cause of the poor is one thing and carrying out the sentence of the court is its sequel.

Examine now, as poetry, the simplest form of synonymous parallelism, where a superb proverb says the same thing twice.

> A just balance and scales are the Lord's;
>   all the weights in the bag are his work   (16:11).

Christians have been known to move heaven and earth to discover different significances between the two halves of such a verse. Christians likewise have been known to take the precept into their hearts. All the essential information is conveyed in the first line; is the second therefore superfluous? It provides harmony and balance. It gives poetic integrity to thought that, despite its theological urgency, has sometimes eluded Christians. The poetic expression makes the thought memorable. That is how it became incorporated in the Bible—somebody remembered it.

The poetic form of parallelism may help us understand the book's title, *The Proverbs of Solomon,* the question to be examined in the next chapter. The usual folk-proverb, in Hebrew as in English, has one line; for example, "As the man is, so is his strength" (Judg. 8:21). Most of the proverbs we are considering have passed through the minds of literary giants. (If you have any doubt about that statement, just try to rephrase a few English proverbs in parallel structure.) Possibly Solomon helped to develop the parallel couplet form of proverb among the Hebrews, and in time any maxim expressed in this way was known as a "proverb of Solomon."

You will readily discover examples of parallelism that combine two of the three forms mentioned, and others that fit none of them precisely. Those who composed the proverbs were not trying to fulfill critical categories invented centuries after their time; they were trying to help their neighbors in the always difficult and the only rewarding task in life, the daily walk with God.

C. S. Lewis, speaking of parallelism, said:

> It is (according to one's point of view) either a wonderful piece of luck or a wise provision of God's, that poetry which was to be turned into all languages should have as its chief formal characteristic one that does not disappear (as mere meter does) in translation.[1]

When you open Proverbs at random, for example to chapter 12, your first and correct impression is that each proverb is independent of what goes before and what follows after, just as the pearls in a necklace are independent of one another. The unity is provided by a thought that runs through the entire book:

> The fear of the Lord is the beginning of knowledge;
> fools despise wisdom and instruction   (1:7).

A closer examination shows that the book as it has come to us is a collection of booklets that may have circulated independently for years or centuries until they were brought together, perhaps by the men of Hezekiah (25:1).

The first nine chapters are an exquisite booklet in praise of wisdom. The tenth chapter introduces the next booklet (10:1—22:16) by repeating the title, "The Proverbs of Solomon." The early King James Version summarizes, in a delightful way, the content of this booklet as "sundry observations of morall vertues, and their contrary vices." A little further subdividing is possible. In chapters 10 through 15 most of the disconnected proverbs point out in contrasted parallelism the great contrast of good and evil. From 16:1 to the end of the booklet, proverbs in constructive parallelism abound. For example:

---

1. C. S. Lewis, *Reflections on the Psalms* (New York: Harcourt, Brace & Company, 1964), p. 4.

Commit your work to the Lord,
    and your plans will be established   (16:3).

In this section of the booklet you find more connection between individual proverbs than in the preceding. The first nine verses of chapter 16, for example, emphasize God's ultimate control over all human activity.

Proverbs 22:17 says, "Incline your ear and hear the words of the wise." The booklet thus introduced consists largely of stanzas with four or six lines, rather than couplets. This short booklet is a thoughtful and remarkably thorough manual of conduct.

The next change in style is introduced, "These also are the sayings of the wise" (24:23). A few sentences in this brief section are not in poetry.

A booklet comprising 125 verses begins, "These also are proverbs of Solomon which the men of Hezekiah king of Judah copied" (25:1). Here are many groupings of proverbs by subject matter. One portion emphasizes the king, another the sluggard, another fools, and a superb section social pests.

Three short booklets complete Proverbs: the words of Agur, son of Jakeh (30:1–33); the words of Lemuel, king of Massa, which his mother taught him (31:1–9); and an incredibly lovely poem, The Courageous Woman (31:10–31).

As you examine the different booklets you will not find the majestic progression of thought that fills the Book of Job or Paul's Letter to the Romans. The differences between the booklets are chiefly in literary style; in content they are remarkably similar. They uphold the same noble virtues: reverence to God, respect for parents, family solidarity and love, industry, thrift, honesty, compassion. They warn against the same evils: sexual promiscuity, sloth, folly, cruelty, falsehood. The booklets differ in form of expression, but they are bound together by one basic thought:

In all your ways acknowledge him,
    and he will make straight your paths   (3:6).

I have suggested three angles from which you might examine the proverbs. You might attempt to classify them by content, you might analyze their poetic form, and you might try to improve on my outline of the book. I have likewise suggested that you will never reach the end of your task, because Proverbs is highly resistant to classification, but you will gain much wisdom and insight as you work at it.

You will find in Proverbs many passages that do not fit our idea of a proverb. You will find a few verses that impress you as being cynical, on a spiritual level with "You can't fight city hall." You will find several that puzzle you; just what is the writer getting at (e.g., 18:1)? You will find exceptions to any general statement I make about the book. More important, you will find in its pages a great deal of warm, friendly counsel about the problems you and your family face. Knowing the Book of Proverbs will help you walk with God.

2

The Wise

Who wrote the Book of Proverbs? The answer is not so clear-cut as you might gather from the title line, "The proverbs of Solomon, son of David, king of Israel" (1:1). The possessive case, in Hebrew as in English, is ambiguous; the title might mean that Solomon composed all that follows, or it might not. Since we have two other named authors, Agur (30:1) and Lemuel (31:1), we conclude that Solomon did not write the entire book. About Agur and his father Jakeh we know nothing beyond the cryptic words of 30:1; *agur* may mean "collector." Lemuel, whose name means "devoted, belonging to God," is unknown; in any case, we have his mother's teaching, not Lemuel's.

I believe the answer to the question about authorship is found in one of the booklet introductions mentioned in the previous chapter. "These also are the sayings of the wise" (24:23). "The wise" is plural. Who were the wise? We have mentioned Agur and Lemuel's mother; then there were "the men of Hezekiah."

A passage in the Talmud, written about the fourth century, says "King Hezekiah and his company wrote Isaiah, Proverbs, The Song, and Ecclesiastes" (*Baba bathra*, 152). King Hezekiah himself was a poet (Isa. 38:10–20). During his reign a body of scribes must have engaged in significant editorial labors; for their activity in producing Proverbs we have only the tantalizing information, "These also are proverbs of Solomon which the men of Hezekiah king of Judah copied" (25:1).

The other named author of Proverbs, about whom we know a great deal more, is Solomon. Much of what we know about him does not fit our concept of a wise man. However, the Holy Bible presents the founders of our faith in perspective, with their many faults and with their virtues. In the case of Solomon, we read:

> He had seven hundred wives, princesses, and three hundred concubines; and his wives turned away his heart. For when Solomon was old his wives turned away his heart after other gods; and his heart was not wholly true to the Lord his God (I Kings 11:3–4).

In defense of this marital nightmare, it can be said that with Solomon marriage was an instrument of diplomacy. When one of the neighboring kings thought of making war against him the court scribe would warn, "Your majesty, Solomon is your son-in-law." I do not praise this policy beyond pointing out that, in combination with other factors, it was highly successful. During Solomon's forty-year reign (I Kings 11:42), his land knew blessed peace. In the maelstrom of Middle-eastern politics, great skill was (and is) required to keep the ship of state afloat, and Solomon succeeded at this difficult task for forty long years.

Solomon's political success verges on the miraculous when you consider that during his reign gold mining was highly developed (I Kings 9:28). Gold evokes a passionate response, today as yesterday. The miracle is that one of the powerful nations, Assyria or Egypt, did not move in and seize the mines. Instead, they left to Solomon the difficult work of removing the gold; then, by one means and another, they took it away from his successors (I Kings 14:15–16; II Kings 16–25).

Solomon's reign was marked by peace and fantastic prosperity (I Kings 10–12). He maintained a magnificent court. The Hebrews looked back upon his time as the "golden age" in every sense of the term. His rule brought great wealth (for the wealthy), high scholarship, and peace. When Jesus pictured dazzling beauty, he referred to "Solomon in all his glory" (Matt. 6:29). May our knowledge of Solomon's many weaknesses never blind us to his political achievement. He built what his successors were unable to maintain. Political art requires just as much wisdom as any other fine art. Great rulers are at least as rare in world history as are great poets and great sculptors. The Bible says of Solomon:

> God gave Solomon wisdom and understanding beyond measure, and largeness of mind like the sand on the seashore, so that Solomon's wisdom surpassed the wisdom of all the people of the east, and all the wisdom of Egypt. For he was wiser than all other men, wiser than Ethan the Ezrahite, and Heman, Calcol, and Darda, the sons of Mahol; and his fame was in all the nations round about. He also uttered three thousand proverbs; and his songs were a thousand and five. He spoke of trees, from the cedar that is in Lebanon to the hyssop that grows out of the wall; he spoke also of beasts, and of birds, and of reptiles, and of fish. And men came from all peoples to hear the wisdom of Solomon, and from all the kings of the earth, who had heard of his wisdom (I Kings 4:29–34).

Solomon composed three thousand proverbs. We must remember that, when a king produced a zircon of wisdom, his courtiers would acclaim it as a diamond. Most of the three thousand, in the wisdom of the Holy Spirit, are lost. I believe that Solomon was a man of ready wit who could turn a phrase with the best. Along with the semiprecious stones in his jewel case of proverbs, I believe there were some of gem quality which were incorporated into the Book of Proverbs. I can picture him dashing off aphorisms about industry, thrift, and the other virtues of citizenship. I can picture him expressing concisely and forcibly such a political thought as:

> A wise king winnows the wicked,
>   and drives the wheel over them   (20:26).

I can likewise readily believe that Solomon composed some barbed comments about women and marriage that men still consider very funny (e.g., 25:24). Certainly he was in a position to know everything that can go wrong in married life. But his experience largely disqualified him to express the compassionate wisdom about family love, the proverbs on which this essay is focused. Instead, the record shows that Solomon spoke of trees, beasts, birds, reptiles, fish; most of the remaining proverbs dealing with these matters are attributed to Agur, not Solomon (30:18–19, 24–28, 29–31). "God gave Solomon wisdom and understanding," true. It does not follow that he understood everything.

With uncharacteristic humility, biblical critics do not attempt to separate the proverbs composed by Solomon, himself, from those composed by others and incorporated into the book. I suggested in the previous chapter that "the proverbs of Solomon" may refer to the artistic form of expression: couplets in poetic parallelism. If so, the situation is comparable with that of King James, who fancied himself an author. We in the United States remember his name because during his reign others produced the incomparable translation of the Bible we call the King James Version. My real concern, in any case, is not who wrote this or that verse, but what the verse means to us.

In addition to Agur, Lemuel's mother, Solomon, and the men of Hezekiah, I believe there were several hundred other human authors of Proverbs—the "wise," whose names are recorded in the Lamb's Book of Life, not yet available for our inspection. They have left us the record of their work. They were not zealous to promote their own fame; their desire was to help us to walk each day with God. Who were the "wise"?

The biblical record exalts Solomon's wisdom above that of Ethan, Heman, Calcol, and Darda. Possibly the former two are mentioned in the titles of Psalms 88 and 89; we know nothing of the other two. But the record goes on to mention with respect "the wisdom of all the people of the east and all the wisdom of Egypt." The biblical tradition of wisdom is placed with, though above, that of the surrounding nations.

Long before God spoke to Abraham, thoughtful people asked the basic questions of life. Scholars have discovered a highly developed wisdom tradition among the Sumerians, who invented writing. We must suppose that, for thousands of years before it was possible to write it down, people were searching for wisdom about family life and other important matters, expressing their thoughts in memorable form.

Those in many lands who found and expressed workable answers to puzzling questions were called the wise, and the Bible honors them (e.g., Jer. 49:7–22, where the prophet cries that divine judgment is coming because Edom has forsaken wisdom; see also Obad. 8; Jer. 50:35; 51:57). So great is the respect for non-Hebrew wisdom that the words of the wise (22:17–23:12) are taken from the Egyptian *Book of Amen-em-ope* with only insignificant changes. Christians will always revere the wise men from the East (Matt. 2:1–12). We accept wisdom from non-Christian sources, such as the profound truth that six times eight equals forty-eight. Thus it is not surprising that our Hebrew forebears recognized wisdom when it arose in other cultures.

The biblical word for "wise" is *chakam*. The Bible's first use of the term is the seductive encounter in the Garden of Eden, where we learn that the pursuit of wisdom is perilous (Gen. 3:1–7). The next mention is Joseph's encounter with the wise men of Egypt. If these had been considered mountebanks or charlatans, Joseph's victory over them would have been hollow. It was the highest praise when Pharaoh said to Joseph, "There is none so discreet and wise as you are" (Gen. 41:39).

At the minimum, "wisdom" means "technical proficiency." Biblical wisdom has no place for the "wise fool" in modern society, with a Ph.D. but no ability to practice his knowledge. The tailors and seamstresses who fashioned Aaron's robe were "wise of heart" (Exod. 28:3), as were the goldsmiths who toiled with Bezalel (Exod. 31:6), and the women who spun goats' hair threads for the tent of meeting (Exod. 35:25). (In each case the RSV translation is "ability.") Military proficiency is called "wisdom" (Isa. 10:13); as is good seamanship (Ezek. 27:8). The phrase "they were at their wits' end" is literally "their wisdom was swallowed up" (Psalm 107:27). The women who led the mourning were "wise" (Jer. 9:17; RSV translates "skillful"). Their function was not merely to make a doleful racket; we who try to bring the consolation of faith and human friendship know that it takes wisdom in every sense to help mourners.

Wisdom never lost its practical foundations in biblical

thought. The Hebrews were a practical nation; they had to be. From their beginnings, they and their neighbors knew a class of "elders" (Gen. 50:7), who administered civil affairs and played a significant part in religious life. Some, at least, of the elders came to be called "the wise." These developed into a recognized class within Hebrew society who sought the good life and taught their neighbors how to achieve it.

The first biblical person in the Bible to be given the title "wise" was a woman of Tekoa whose counsel influenced the king (II Sam. 14:1–20). The savage story recorded in II Samuel 20: 14–22 tells of another wise woman. Probably the wise developed, as a class, from the scribes or writers who are prominent in the New Testament. Among Solomon's high officials, Elihoreph and Ahijah, the scribes, are mentioned in the place of honor, directly after the high priest (I Kings 4:3).

The prophet Isaiah, in the eighth century B.C., mentions a class of teachers called "the wise." He comments acidly that their teaching, by rote, passed through the students' mouths but not through their hearts, and he warns, "the wisdom of their wise men shall perish" (Isa. 29:13–14). A century later, the prophet Jeremiah used the terms "wise" and "scribe" interchangeably (Jer. 8:8–9). More significant, Jeremiah put the "counsel" of the wise on a level with the "law" of the priest or the "word" of the prophet (Jer. 18:18); that is, the best of wisdom speaks with the voice of God. Ezekiel, likewise joining the three groups of religious leaders, mentions the prophet, the priest, and "the counsel of the elders" (Ezek. 7:26).

The prophets cried "thus said the Lord," and in His name they spoke judgment or salvation. The priests guarded and interpreted the Torah, the divinely given law. The wise did not emphasize the divine authority of their counsel. Rather, these quizzical, thoughtful, practical men and women looked at the basic experience of life and recorded what they saw.

> The father of the righteous will greatly rejoice;
>   he who begets a wise son will be glad in him   (23:24).

This is one of many statements of observed fact; it is not admonition or instruction. It is but a short step from statement to admonition, and the wise often took this step.

Let your father and mother be glad,
   let her who bore you rejoice (23:25).

Just as the scientist today observes the bewildering phenomena of nature and attempts to discern significant relationships, the wise observed, from generation to generation, and expressed their observations in memorable phrases. The Hebrews were not the only ones to notice that pride is the forerunner of disaster; the Greek tragedies are based on the same theme. But the connection has never been more succinctly expressed than by the proverb:

Pride goes before destruction
   and a haughty spirit before a fall (16:18; see also 18:12).

It took brilliant, probing minds to find a relationship between gravity and electricity; it took similar discernment to discover that pride, which appears the basis of all achievement, ultimately destroys itself.

The wise delighted in paradox. To discover and express a truth that appears contradictory is a form of mastering life; underlying the surface confusion is a basic world order.

Bread gained by deceit is sweet to a man,
   but afterward his mouth will be full of gravel (20:17).

He who is kind to the poor lends to the Lord,
   and he will repay him for his deed (19:17).

What is immediately advantageous is not always truly beneficial. It is wisdom to discern the underlying order, and thereby guide your life.

The pursuit of knowledge must always be with a humble reverence for the facts, a deep knowledge of human limitation.

Do you see a man who is wise in his own eyes?
   there is more hope for a fool than for him (26:12).

The "fool," the living denial of wisdom, appears more often in the Book of Proverbs than in all the rest of the Bible. The biblical fool may have an excellent brain but he lacks essential direction. A wisdom psalm begins, "The fool says in his heart, 'There is no God'" (Ps. 14:1). The ensuing picture shows that fools may make a lot of money; they "eat up my people as they eat bread" (Ps. 14:4). The wisest of the wise pictured the fool as a successful business man (Luke 12:16–20). Jesus asked the burning question about the goal of our striving, when He refined the thought of His wise predecessors, "What is a man profited if he shall gain the whole world, and lose his own soul?" (Matt. 16:26, KJV).

If "the fear of the Lord is the beginning of wisdom" (9:10), then the beginning of folly is irreverence for God and contempt for His teaching.

> He who trusts in his own mind is a fool,
> but he who walks in wisdom will be delivered   (28:26).

The fool lacks humility. He pits his judgment against the wisdom of his people and against God. Like his counterpart in the modern proverb, he rushes in where angels fear to tread. He disregards the discipline by which a wise person is guided.

> The vexation of a fool is known at once,
> but the prudent man ignores an insult   (12:16).
>
> A fool takes no pleasure in understanding
> but only in expressing his opinion   (18:2).

The walk in wisdom differs in one significant respect from today's scientific pursuit of truth. The scientist, ideally, begins with no presupposition beyond the great leap of faith that tomorrow nature and mathematics will behave as they did yesterday. The wise, in ancient time, accepted that the primary fact of experience is God.

> The fear of the Lord is the beginning of wisdom,
> and the knowledge of the Holy One is insight   (9:10).
>
> No wisdom, no understanding, no counsel,
> can avail against the Lord.
> The horse is made ready for the day of battle
> but the victory belongs to the Lord   (21:30–31).

In another respect the wise in biblical time differed from contemporary thinkers; they did not formulate vast systems. They did not know the magnificent abstractions of Platonic and Aristotelian thought. We Christians ought to be able to see the danger of systematic thought; in our fierce passion to reduce everything to dogma, we bend uncomfortable facts into shapes that fit comfortably into our systems. The wise, unlike us, accepted the given fact with reverence; if two facts of experience appeared to contradict one another the wise expressed both.

> Answer not a fool according to his folly,
>   lest you be like him yourself.
> Answer a fool according to his folly,
>   lest he be wise in his own eyes   (26:4–5).

The wise observed, expressed their observation pithily, and passed their wisdom on to others. Egyptian wisdom, like that of ancient China, was chiefly for students preparing to become officials. Obviously instruction for young courtiers was a part of Hebrew wisdom; read chapters 25–29 with attention to the political proverbs. You could not formulate a systematic philosophy of government from these chapters, but the world you live in would be a much happier place if the wisdom expressed therein were practiced in Washington, Capetown, Moscow, and other important capital cities. But the focus of Proverbs is not upon an official class; the divine Word speaks to our common human condition. We find something about affairs of state, but mostly we discover pungent epigrams about buying and selling, relationships with the neighbors, the right and the wrong use of speech, the glorious and sometimes difficult relationship between husband and wife, the problems of growing up, and those of raising a family.

There is a great deal that we do not know about the wise. Were they officially recognized? Did they pass examinations and receive degrees? Did they—as a few proverbs seem to indicate (e.g., 17:16)—receive fees for their teaching? Did they have some sort of organization comparable to the schools of the prophets or the intricate orders of priesthood? Were all the scribes called wise, or just those who deserved it? These questions we cannot answer. We have seen that a group of highly respected people gave a kind of spiritual-political-economic leadership that was not provided by the priests or the prophets. They did not seek self-glory as individuals or as a class. They just tried to help their neighbors—and you—to walk each day with God.

From the time of the judges until the Maccabean period, sages taught, usually at the city gate. Unlike the prophets who usually began their majestic oracles, "Thus saith the Lord," the wise began their counsel, "Hear, my son," or with something comparable. You will find it profitable to read through Proverbs, marking each occurrence of the term, "my son." If you read with care, you will decide that this was a linguistic convention which could, with propriety, mean "my daughter."

The Book of Proverbs is introduced:

> Hear, my son, your father's instruction,
>   and reject not your mother's teaching   (1:8).

No other book in the Holy Bible emphasizes as does Proverbs the love and respect that are due to a mother. She is honored for her vital part in transmitting wisdom to the family. Presumably she acquired some of her wisdom in girlhood from a teacher who gravely addressed her as "my son."

The teacher, the wise one, sat with his students at the city gate and imparted wisdom, hoping and praying that the young people who listened would remember and apply what they had learned, in the courtroom and the legislature, in the market place, in the sweat-soaked fields, and most important of all, in the home. The teacher's purpose is summarized:

> That men may know wisdom and instruction,
>   understand words of insight,
> receive instruction in wise dealing,
>   righteousness, justice, and equity;
> that prudence may be given to the simple,
>   knowledge and discretion to the youth—
> the wise man also may hear and increase in learning,
>   and the man of understanding acquire skill,
> to understand a proverb and a figure,
>   the words of the wise and their riddles.
> The fear of the Lord is the beginning of knowledge;
>   fools despise wisdom and instruction   (1:2–7).

The father and mother who were not entitled "the wise," passed on the traditions of the elders, partly through the proverbs they had learned as children, and more important through practicing what they had learned.

We find a superb picture of a wise man, though the term is not used, as Job looks back from the ash heap upon his days of leadership. Job, you recall, was a farmer, not a professional scholar or jurist. You will discern in this picture no ivory tower isolation; Job lived his wisdom.

> When I went out to the gate of the city,
>   when I prepared my seat in the square,
> the young men saw me and withdrew,
>   and the aged rose and stood;
> the princes refrained from talking,
>   and laid their hand on their mouth;
> the voice of the nobles was hushed,
>   and their tongue cleaved to the roof of their mouth.
> When the ear heard, it called me blessed,
>   and when the eye saw, it approved;
> because I delivered the poor who cried,
>   and the fatherless who had none to help him.
> The blessing of him who was about to perish came upon me,
>   and I caused the widow's heart to sing for joy.
> I put on righteousness, and it clothed me;
>   my justice was like a robe and a turban.
> I was eyes to the blind,
>   and feet to the lame.
> I was a father to the poor,
>   and I searched out the cause of him whom I did not know.
> I broke the fangs of the unrighteous,
>   and made him drop his prey from his teeth.
> Then I thought, "I shall die in my nest,
>   and I shall multiply my days as the sand,
> my roots spread out to the waters,
>   with the dew all night on my branches,
> my glory fresh with me,
>   and my bow ever new in my hand."
> Men listened to me, and waited,
>   and kept silence for my counsel.
> After I spoke they did not speak again,
>   and my word dropped upon them.
> They waited for me as for the rain;
>   and they opened their mouths as for the spring rain.
> I smiled on them when they had no confidence;

and the light of my countenance they did not cast down.
I chose their way, and sat as chief,
   and I dwelt like a king among his troops,
   like one who comforts mourners (Job 29:7–25).

Centuries later, another writer described the wise man of his time, who was not a farmer but a professional scholar and theologian. Otherwise, the differences between the two pictures are superficial. Each of the wise practiced his faith and taught his followers to live by wisdom.

It is not so with the man who applies himself,
And studies the Law of the Most High.
He searches out the wisdom of all the ancients,
And busies himself with prophecies;
He observes the discourse of famous men,
And penetrates the intricacies of figures.
He searches out the hidden meaning of proverbs,
And acquaints himself with the obscurities of figures.
He will serve among great men,
And appear before rulers.
He will travel through the lands of strange peoples,
And test what is good and what is evil among men.
He will devote himself to going early
To the Lord his Maker,
And will make his entreaty before the Most High.
He will open his mouth in prayer,
And make entreaty for his sins.
If the great Lord pleases,
He will be filled with the spirit of understanding,
He will pour out his wise sayings,
And give thanks to the Lord in prayer;
He will direct his counsel and knowledge,
And study his secrets.
He will reveal instruction in his teaching,
and will glory in the Law of the Lord's agreement.
Many will praise his understanding,
And it will never be blotted out.
His memory will not disappear,
And his name will live for endless generations.
Nations will repeat his wisdom,
And the congregation will utter his praise.
If he lives long, he will leave a greater name than a thousand,
And if he goes to rest, his fame is enough for him.[1]

1. Ecclesiasticus 39:1–11 *The Apocrypha; An American Translation*, Edgar J. Goodspeed (Chicago; The University of Chicago Press, 1938).

The wise produced some of the most fascinating books ever written. The Book of Job, the incomparable examination of faith in the flames, is at the pinnacle of wisdom (and all other) literature. You will emerge a better Christian if you wrestle your way through Ecclesiastes, where you will find your doubts brought, without mercy(?), to the surface. Psalm 1, and several others are called "wisdom psalms." There are two examples of wisdom literature in the Apocrypha that strongly influenced the New Testament writers, and are worthy of your intensive examination. One is the Wisdom of Solomon, written in Greek between 50 B.C. and 40 B.C. to help the Hebrews in Egypt in their battles of faith. (It will help you in your battles.) The other is Ecclesiasticus, which was originally composed in Hebrew about 180 B.C., and then translated into Greek. You will benefit greatly from reading this book; many parts of it are on a level with the noblest parts of Proverbs.

Each of these books has great value; I commend each to you. I believe that James included all of them when he spoke of "the wisdom from above" (James 3:17). Incidentally, the Epistle of James has been called the last of the great Wisdom Literature. But this essay is not about Wisdom Literature, it concerns what Proverbs has to say about family life. Henceforth, I refer to other Wisdom Literature only to illustrate what Proverbs teaches.

Who were the human authors of Proverbs? Agur and the mother of Lemuel, to be sure. The men of Hezekiah, you may believe, did more than "copy." Think of Solomon, witty and debonaire, and give him all possible credit; he did compose some of the "Proverbs of Solomon." But when you picture the human authors of a divine book, think primarily of a farmer, or a farmer's wife, who toiled and thought during the long day, then, in the evening, went to the place of instruction and passed on dedicated thought to young people, to friends and neighbors, and to you and your family.

3

Wisdom

The wise composed the Book of Proverbs to help you and your family in the pursuit of wisdom. Considerately they devoted the first third of their book to this elusive thing you are pursuing. The focus of their introduction is upon the God-centered home. Here in the opening chapters the teacher gives a brief glimpse of his own childhood, where he learned the rudiments of wisdom from his parents. Here is one of the most beautiful songs ever sung in praise of marital love. Here is a warning, many times repeated, against the dangers of sexual promiscuity. The introduction says directly:

> Happy is the man who finds wisdom,
>   and the man who gets understanding,
> for the gain from it is better than gain from silver
>   and its profit better than gold   (3:13–14).

Many times over the introduction says that the best place to acquire wisdom is within a God-centered home, and that the most important function of a God-centered home is to impart wisdom.

The word "wisdom" (chokmah), comes from chakam "to be wise," which first meant "fasten, hold fast"; then it came to mean "separate, decide." Wisdom is right decision about conduct made by holding fast to God and his law. It is knowing and following the right way, avoiding the wrong.

The introduction to the Introduction (1:2–7) can serve as a definition of wisdom, or at least an outline of its boundaries. Notice how many terms are grouped together to illustrate different aspects of wisdom: instruction, insight, wise dealing, righteousness, justice, equity, prudence, knowledge, discretion, learning, understanding, skill, and then, summing them all together, "the fear of the Lord."

The closest English equivalent to wisdom that I know is the old-fashioned term "gumption" which my grandmother used, generally with heated reference to my lack thereof. Gumption, as my grandmother used the term, has two components: knowing what to do, and doing it when it needs to be done. Energy, not guided by intellect, she called "brute strength." Knowledge without action she called "book larnin'." Although the wise elders who composed Proverbs did not use her language, they developed the distinction.

The editor of Proverbs, whose name we will not know until we meet in heaven, first outlines the basic theme of the book and then gravely advises "my son" (meaning you and me), to avoid the total denial of wisdom, the foolishness of armed robbery. The details of vicious crime have changed, though not much, during the past few millennia. But the end result remains exactly what it was when a wise person wrote:

These men lie in wait for their own blood,
they set an ambush for their own lives   (1:18).

The Revised Standard Version translation of verse 19, "such are the ways of all who get gain by violence," misses the point. The verb in question, *batsa'*, basically means "cut off parts or pieces." Under some circumstances it can mean "wound"; so the translation "by violence" is defensible grammatically, if not psychologically. The derived meaning of the verb is "acquire gain." Proverbs never disparages honest reward for honest labor, but *batsa'* almost always has overtones of greed. A better translation is:

So are the ways of every one that is greedy of gain;
which taketh away the life of the owners thereof (1:19, KJV).

Do you see what our wise teacher has done? First he exalted wisdom and had us sagely nodding. How true, how true. Then he pointed out with clarity the destructive effect of crime, and still we nodded in total agreement. You and I have no intention of committing armed robbery. Then the elder lowered the boom on us. He wasn't really talking about criminals but about us greedy people. I know that I am greedy, and I strongly suspect that you are, too; and greed is deadly. The wise teacher shows us something we wouldn't dream about, violent crime. Then with compassion—for he too is a sinner—he says, "Thou art the man" (II Sam. 12:7, KJV). Proverbs frequently does this: first you have the comfortable feeling that the discussion concerns somebody else; then you discover, all of a sudden, that it's aimed at you. (Read I John 3:11–15 with this teaching technique in mind.)

Following the basic outline of the subject and the admonition that the message is intended for you, Wisdom, personified, calls. She sings a brief song (1:22–23) that is enriched a thousandfold in chapter 8. Notice that in contrast with the secret enticing of the evil-doers (1:10), she "cries aloud in the street; in the markets she raises her voice; on the top of the walls she cries out." Wisdom calls to the world, not to an esoteric band of disciples. She invites "simple ones," "scoffers," and "fools," those who "have ignored all my counsel and would have none of my reproof."

We have encountered the "fool" (of either gender) and we shall meet again in Proverbs, frequently (58 times more). The "simple," likewise abound. The root verb *pathach* means "open" (31:9); a cognate noun means "door" (5:8). The simple person, the wide-open one, is undecided in his views; he is susceptible to every influence; he desperately needs old-fashioned prudence, which is a major ingredient of wisdom (8:12).

The simple believes everything,
but the prudent looks where he is going   (14:15).

Scoffers have not disappeared from the earth; Psalm 1:1 urges us to avoid their company. The word *lutz*, "scorn," occurs twenty times in Proverbs (e.g., 20:1), only ten times in the rest of the Old Testament, and four of these occurrences have the related meaning "interpreter." (Now that's an interesting association in ideas, isn't it? You may be sure that it rankles in the mind of one who is attempting to interpret Proverbs.)

Wisdom warns that those who ignore her counsel will surely bring disaster upon themselves, but her warning ends on a warm, positive note.

> Then they will call upon me, but I will not answer;
>   they will seek me diligently but will not find me.
> For the simple are killed by their turning away,
>   and the complacence of fools destroys them;
> but he who listens to me will dwell secure
>   and will be at ease, without dread of evil   (1:28, 32–33).

Following Wisdom's brief song are two chapters in which the elder shows the happy result of accepting wisdom. He teaches that

> if you seek it like silver
>   and search for it as for hidden treasures;
> then you will understand the fear of the Lord
>   and find the knowledge of God.
> For the Lord gives wisdom;
>   from his mouth come knowledge and understanding   (2:4–6).

Compare the boundaries of wisdom as given in 1:2–7 with the catalogue in 2:1–11: commandments, understanding, insight, fear of the Lord, knowledge of God, sound wisdom (a different word, *tushiyah*, "practical sense"), integrity, righteousness, justice, equity, knowledge, and discretion.

Wisdom is practiced not in a vacuum, but in this rough and tumble world filled with delicious temptations that make it difficult to be wise. The elder, with discerning impartiality, warns against evil men (2:12–15) and against the loose woman (2:16–19). In his warning against "men whose paths are crooked," he gives only one specific: they are "men of perverted speech"; their talking is literally "upside down." A medieval rabbi suggested, with considerable plausibility, that

upside down talking means the philosophy that the only good
is physical pleasure; a thought that has not disappeared from
the world.

You can understand the warning against the loose woman on
two levels of meaning. Adultery is a bitter metaphor for
idolatry in the prophetic writings (Hos. 1–3; Jer. 2–3; etc.).
Many Canaanite religions had the hideous practice of cultic
prostitution; Hebrew women who turned to the cult of Astarte
would sell themselves and call it religion. Ezekiel, in a ghastly
chapter where harlotry symbolizes idolatry, seems to say that
even in Jerusalem cultic prostitutes sold their bodies (Ezek.
16:25). So harlotry was both a symbol for infidelity to God and
an expression of that infidelity. On this level of meaning the
teaching of the elder has great historical interest but not much
practical relevance; only the more subtle forms of vice come
masked as religion today. Without denying the symbolism of
the loose woman, I believe that uppermost in the elder's mind
as he taught was the ever-present temptation to sexual promiscuity in the literal sense. There is nothing new about the new
morality; it was old before ancient Sodom was built. The loose
woman pictured in Proverbs is an adulteress who has "forsaken
the companion of her youth." Her picture is painted again in
5:3–6 with even more acerbity, and at greater length in 7:5–27.
In each case the conclusion is much the same:

> Her house sinks down to death,
>   and her paths to the shades (2:18).

The elder's address continues with a bit more than the
synonymous parallelism that is obvious:

> My son, do not forget my teaching,
>   but let your heart keep my commandments (3:1).

"My commandments" means the counsel of the wise, but this is
linked with *torah*, "teaching," which is usually translated
"law." The Jewish people today call the heart of the Scripture
the Torah. It is God's Word. The elder made it his own, and the
Torah became "my teaching." The essence of the divine-human
counsel is:

4. In all your ways acknowledge him,
   and he will make straight your paths   (3:6).

The next thought grates on the Christian reader:

Honor the Lord with your substance,
  and with the first fruits of all your produce;
then your barns will be filled with plenty,
  and your vats will be bursting with wine   (3:9–10).

The conclusion is disturbing; it points to a material result from virtuous action. This disturbance will rise, frequently, as you read through Proverbs. If indeed, you "honor the Lord with your substance" in order that "your vats will be bursting with wine," you have not very subtly turned your faith into a moneymaking gimmick like a new computer or a hot tip on the stock market. We shall look at this aspect of Proverbs again.

A short interlude (3:11–12) anticipates an inevitable question. "But Teacher, many good people don't prosper. What do you say to all the pain in the world? Godly people suffer. Innocent children starve. What do you say?" The interlude, which closely parallels the answers given to Job by his friends, Eliphaz (Job 4–5; 15; 22) and Elihu (Job 32–37), points to God's "discipline," *musar.* This term occurs more often in Proverbs than in all the rest of the Bible. Its many shades of meaning in Hebrew are brought out by the principal English translations: chastisement, discipline, instruction, correction. When adversity is accepted as "tuning of my breast, to make the music better," it leads me to correct what needs to be corrected, and draws me to God. When I defy God's discipline, I confirm myself in evil. The Book of Job demonstrates that this, or any answer in words, is only partially true. God's final answer to the questions raised by pain is the cross.

The interlude concludes with one of the most profound thoughts in the Bible, which bears directly upon the theme of this essay:

The Lord reproves [a different verb] him whom he loves,
  as a father the son in whom he delights   (3:12; see also Ps. 119:71).

Mull over the implications. God is trying—sometimes with little visible success—to help me grow into the likeness of Christ. For many years of my life, His principal influence on me was through my parents. I badly needed reproof when I was a child. Looking back on those days, I see that representatives of God, my parents, were trying to teach me wisdom because they loved me. When in turn I became a father, I discovered that children are not perpetually cute and cuddly; on occasion I must show my love for them and for God, by *musar*. God made me an earthly father to represent my heavenly Father in raising our children. Me? God's representative? It's a staggering thought, and the answer is "Yes." You represent God. When you bring a child into this world you continue his miracle of creation. When you "train up a child in the way he should go" (22:6), you are God's chosen agent of salvation.

After the short digression the theme resumes: the one who finds wisdom is "happy." The particular benefits mentioned are long life, riches, honor, pleasantness, and peace. Once more the grating on our sensibilities; however great our zeal in pursuing wealth, we don't like to have the Bible mention it. We think that the Bible ought to be more "spiritual." In this case the elder is warning us to put our materialism into proper focus. He says that Wisdom

> is more precious than jewels
> and nothing you desire can compare with her (3:15).

Wisdom's work in creation (3:19–20) is developed in 8:22–31. At the creation God brought order from the primordial chaos; the function of wisdom in family life is similar. The one who keeps sound wisdom and discretion knows security (3:23), freedom from fear (3:24–25), confidence, and deliverance (3:26).

The concluding section of chapter 3 is markedly different in style and content from what precedes and what follows. It is similar to most of Proverbs, individual thoughts are expressed with no logical connection. We shall consider some of these thoughts in later chapters, at the moment we are thinking about wisdom.

The fourth chapter is the heart of the essay on wisdom; it contains a priceless picture of a God-centered home (4:3–9). We have pictured the elder at the city gate, with his students gathered around. Here he gives a brief, affection-packed glimpse of his own childhood. Picture the family gathered, the father speaking with love to his children, offering them instruction (*musar*) and insight. He teaches "good precepts." "Precept," *leqach*, comes from the verb "receive." It is not original, it comes from the past, it is tradition. A precept has been tried and it works. The wise, unlike us, thought it better to be right than to be novel; perhaps that is why their teaching is still important.

The elder speaks of his own childhood, when he was "a son with my father, tender, the only one in the sight of my mother." "Only one" is a term of affection, not arithmetic. The elder may well have had a dozen brothers and sisters; in an ideal home each would be the "only one."

> He taught me, and said to me,
> "Let your heart hold fast my words;
>   keep my commandments, and live;
> do not forget, and do not turn away from the words of my mouth.
>   Get wisdom; get insight.
> Do not forsake her, and she will keep you;
>   love her, and she will guard you.
> The beginning of wisdom is this: Get wisdom,
>   and whatever you get, get insight.
> Prize her highly, and she will exalt you;
>   she will honor you if you embrace her.
> She will place on your head a fair garland;
>   she will bestow on you a beautiful crown" (4:4–9).

The verb here, "get," is literally "buy." Its use suggests that the wise may have received fees for their teaching. The possibility should not unduly alarm us; our school teachers are paid. There is no conflict between the father's wise counsel and the same precept in 9:10, "The fear of the Lord is the beginning of wisdom." Biblical wisdom is never isolated from faith, and the faithful are counseled always to be wise. True wisdom will lead inevitably to the source of all wisdom.

Notice the parallelism: verse 5 is expanded in verse 7; verse 6 is expanded in verses 8–9. Picture the father teaching his children the wisdom he received in his childhood. He has come through the stormy years of adolescence. He knows the trials and temptations of maturity. Now he is passing on his greatest treasure to his children, with the prayer that they will pass it on to theirs. A tradition is something received from the past; more, it is passed on to the future.

The address continues with an examination of the paths of good and evil (4:10–19), and concludes with a series of admonitions to follow the good way.

> Take heed to the path of your feet,
>   then all your ways will be sure.
> Do not swerve to the right or to the left;
>   turn your foot away from evil. (4:26–27).

Hebrew, like English, has eight or ten overlapping terms that mean "path, road, way, street." If there is a spiritual distinction among the various Hebrew terms, I have been unable to discern it. But the basic idea of the road, a means of getting from where you are to where you want to go, is found more often in Proverbs than any other biblical book, with Psalms following close behind. Proverbs typically pictures us walking, not riding, along a path. When our feet follow the right way we are blessed; when they go astray, we are in trouble. It is no accident that Jesus said, "I am the way" (John 14:6), or that the early church called herself "the Way" (Acts 9:2).

Chapter 5 illustrates vividly the wrong and the right paths by drawing another contrast between adulterous passion and married love. It is permissible to find here a symbolic meaning, that adultery connotes idolatry and fidelity in marriage means fidelity to God. (Interesting, isn't it, how often the two go together?) But again, I believe the literal interpretation is foremost. This is a warning against sexual adventures of the type that are glorified in the pornographic press, where vice is pictured as pleasure without aftereffects, the normal and natural way to live. The elder recognizes the allure. He says:

> The lips of a loose woman drip honey,
>   and her speech is smoother than oil;

but in the end she is bitter as wormwood,
    sharp as a two-edged sword.
Her feet go down to death;
    her steps follow the path to Sheol (5:3–5).

Since Dr. Kinsey had not conducted his survey in Solomon's time, we have no statistics about marital infidelity. Obviously the elder thought the danger widespread enough for extended comment. I forbear to comment about the danger today.

Of few things am I positive in critical studies of the Bible, but I am positive that Solomon did not write the trenchant, sensitive hymn-poem on marital fidelity (5:15–19) that is the pulsing heartbeat of the chapter. (We shall consider this poem when we examine the teaching of Proverbs about marriage.)

Four warnings against "lack of discipline" (*musar*) follow. Each has a decided bearing upon family life. The first (6:1–5) concerns being "surety for your neighbor." (This matter too, we shall consider in another chapter.)

The second warning, against laziness, is priceless.

Go to the ant, O sluggard;
    consider her ways, and be wise.
Without having any chief,
    officer or ruler,
she prepares her food in summer,
    and gathers her sustenance in harvest.
How long will you lie there, O sluggard?
    When will you arise from your sleep?
A little sleep, a little slumber,
    a little folding of the hands to rest,
and poverty will come upon you like a vagabond,
    and want like an armed man   (6:6–11).

The third warning (6:12–19) concerns "a man who sows discord among brothers." The passage contains a numerical verse of the type that is found many times in the words of Agur (ch. 30), in Job 5:19, and as the introduction to the oracles of judgment in Amos 1–2. This is a teaching device, an aid to the memory. It does not imply an exhaustive catalogue of the "things which the Lord hates." Notice with what skill the elder has mingled the sins you and I would not commit with those of which I, at least, am guilty.

> There are six things which the Lord hates,
>> seven which are an abomination to him:
> haughty eyes, a lying tongue,
>> and hands that shed innocent blood,
> a heart that devises wicked plans,
>> feet that make haste to run to evil,
> a false witness who breathes out lies,
>> and a man who sows discord among brothers   (6:16–19).

The kernel of the chapter is another warning against abusing the sacredness of marriage.

> For the commandment is a lamp and the teaching a light,
>> and the reproofs of discipline are the way of life,
> to preserve you from the evil woman,
>> from the smooth tongue of the adventuress   (6:23–24).

The "smooth tongue of the adventuress" is, literally, "the smoothness of the alien tongue." The elder, I presume, was familiar with the story of Ruth, an alien, who became part of the covenant people. The law commands respect for outsiders (e.g., Exod. 20:10). Solomon's prayer shows compassion for the foreigner (I Kings 8:41–43). Even so, as we have seen, many of the "aliens" who surrounded ancient Israel adored the sex-goddess, who was known by several names; the prophets tearfully warned against her wiles (e.g., Jer. 44). It was bitterly said of Solomon that he loved many foreign women who lured him away from the faith (I Kings 11:1–10). So "alien" here is clearly a term of reproach. In this case, however, the warning is against adultery within the community of faith, not against consorting with harlots who might come from anywhere. Adulterers make themselves "alien" to the covenant.

The line concerning the harlot (6:26) is grammatically difficult. The King James Version translates "by means of a whorish woman a man is brought to a piece of bread," which means that the pursuit of harlots leads to poverty. The Revised Standard Version is, I think, better. The translation shows Christlike sympathy for a lost woman who makes her living the only way she can (see 6:30, RSV footnote). Proverbs speaks of the harlot only rarely (6:26; 7:10; 23:27; 29:3) because the chief danger is adultery. The boy who grows in a God-centered home

looks at the harlot with pity and horror. His sister, whatever
else she may see in her future, shudders at the thought of ever
selling herself. But the enticements of adultery are more subtle;
the warning is sharp, clear, and desperately needed.

> A harlot may be hired for a loaf of bread,
>   but an adulteress stalks a man's very life.
> Can a man carry fire in his bosom
>   and his clothes not be burned?
> Or can one walk upon hot coals
>   and his feet not be scorched?
> So is he who goes in to his neighbor's wife;
>   none who touches her will go unpunished   (6:26–29).

Chapter 7 is a separate discourse, beginning "My son," that
continues and intensifies the thought of the preceding warning. It concerns a married woman "dressed as a harlot" (see
Gen. 38:14–29) and a "simple... young man without sense."
Only one line in the vivid picture of seduction requires comment, the rest might have been written yesterday:

> I had to offer sacrifices,
>   and today I have paid my vows   (7:14).

The flesh of a sacrifice must be eaten on the day of offering or
the following (Lev. 7:15–16). The woman means that she has
food in the house. The practice of turning holy ceremonies to
sordid purposes was, unhappily, quite familiar in ancient times
(e.g., Isa. 1:11, 15; Amos 5:21–22). The conclusion of the matter
is remarkably up-to-date, "He follows her, as an ox goes to the
slaughter."

The warning is addressed to the growing boy. Is his sister an
inert, passionless lump of clay? The elder is addressing her too,
teaching her to say, "There, but for the grace of God, go I." The
necessity for wisdom is not limited to one gender. The elder
teaches the growing girl to follow the good path, with the hope
and prayer that when she is a woman she will continue on the
way that leads to God (22:6).

The elder turns from contemplating the defiled marriage bed
to "the heights beside the way" where Wisdom, personified,
stands and calls:

O simple ones, learn prudence;
  O foolish men, pay attention   (8:5).

You might call a lovely poem (8:12–21) a <u>functional defini-</u><u>tion of wisdom</u>. When a scientist today is examining something too complex to be defined, such as life, he can describe what life does, its outstanding characteristics, how it functions. Here Wisdom shows how she operates in human life, how people become wise, and what they do because they are wise. As always, Wisdom is down to earth.

I, Wisdom, dwell in prudence,
  and I find knowledge and discretion   (8:12).

The English word "<u>prudence</u>" is related to providence: it means exercising foresight, providing, getting ready. Heavenly Wisdom dwells with earthly prudence; she finds "knowledge" and "discretion." Hebrew words have a glorious, and often exasperating, multiplicity of meaning. Other vivid translations for "discretion" are "devices" (AJV), "witty devices" (KJV), "insight" (Moffat), "understanding" (TLB), "judicious knowledge" (NAB). All are human expressions of wisdom, ways in which a wise person acts.

The fear of the Lord is hatred of evil.
  Pride and arrogance and the way of evil
and perverted speech I hate   (8:13).

This verse is not, as some commentators have claimed, an interruption between sentences spoken by Wisdom. It is a subtle affirmation of the basic thesis of the book, that "The fear of the Lord is the beginning of wisdom" (9:10). You might say that verse 12 exalts common sense, erudition, and technology as valid expressions of wisdom. Verse 13 concerns inward attitudes; if you reverence God, you will hate evil. Before you decide that Wisdom is platitudinous, notice the aspects of evil that she hates. It is a rare Christian who cannot find in self at least one of these aspects.

Having told what she hates, Wisdom tells what she delights in.

> I have counsel, and sound wisdom,
>   I have insight, I have strength   (8:14).

The functional definition continues with counsel, sound wisdom, insight, and strength. I personify understanding, says Wisdom, so the one who genuinely understands will give good counsel, will practice "sound wisdom" which, we saw in 2:7, means "practical sense," and will have strength. Practical results flow from genuine understanding. "As he thinketh in his heart, so is he" (23:7, KJV).

Verses 15 and 16 amplify the thought, showing that good government results when rulers are wise. It is interesting to compare these words with Plato's affirmation that the ideal government will be achieved when kings are philosophers. Parents, who have the subtle and immeasurably demanding task of governing a household, likewise require wisdom. Most parents are quick to deny that they are philosophers or sages; they are just ordinary folks who have assumed an overwhelming responsibility. To such people, humbly aware of their needs, Wisdom sings:

> I love those who love me,
>   and those who seek me diligently find me   (8:17).

Wisdom is not limited to those of massive intellect and extended education. Biblical wisdom is for ordinary folks who seek diligently, striving—not always with success—to walk each day with their Lord. Notice the word "diligently." Hebrew, like English, has a number of verbs meaning seek. In this verse is a comparatively rare term, shachar, which can be translated "seek early"; the related noun is "morning." Although the way of wisdom is open to all, not just to the great brains of society, the slothful need not expect to walk thereon.

And now Wisdom, personified, breaks into one of the most beautiful songs in the Bible, a song remarkable both for its poetry and its theological profundity.

> The Lord created me at the beginning of his work,
>   the first of his acts of old.
> Ages ago I was set up,

at the first, before the beginning of the earth.
When there were no depths I was brought forth,
   when there were no springs abounding with water.
Before the mountains had been shaped,
   before the hills, I was brought forth;
before he had made the earth with its fields,
   or the first of the dust of the world.
When he established the heavens, I was there,
   when he drew a circle on the face of the deep,
When he made firm the skies above,
   when he established the fountains of the deep,
when he assigned to the sea its limit,
   so that the waters might not transgress his command,
when he marked out the foundations of the earth,
   then I was beside him, like a master workman;
and I was daily his delight,
   rejoicing before him always,
rejoicing in his inhabited world
   and delighting in the sons of men   (8:22–31).

The Christian reader, thoughtfully examining Wisdom's song about her role in creation, cannot help thinking of John's sublime statement, "In the beginning was the Word, and the Word was with God, and the Word was God" (John 1:1). The resemblance between Wisdom and Christ has occurred to others. In the New Testament, Christ is called the Wisdom of God (Luke 11:49; I Cor. 1:24, 30). John almost certainly had the song from Proverbs in mind when composing the prologue (John 1:1–14); throughout his Gospel John develops the idea that Christ is divine Wisdom. Many, by no means all, Christians see Christ Himself prefigured where Wisdom is personified in the Old Testament.

Christians, forgetting sometimes that Proverbs is poetry, not computer language, have created a great difficulty here. Christians have traditionally affirmed the eternal generation of the Son, that Christ had no beginning. The Arians, in the fourth century, shouted, "There was a time when he was not," and used this passage to support their claim. The council at Nicea, following Athanasius, declared that Christ is "God from God, Light from Light, true God from true God, begotten, not made, one in being with the Father, by whom all things were made." Does this passage support Arius or Athanasius?

41

The debate centers upon the verb *ganah* which the Revised Standard Version, following the Greek Septuagint, translates "created." The verb basically means "acquire," usually, but not necessarily, by purchase. Eve rejoiced, "I have gotten (*ganah*) a man with the help of the Lord" (Gen. 4:1). Moses asked his unruly flock, "Is not he your father who created (*ganah*) you?" (Deut. 32:6). So it does not stretch the meaning of the verb to say that here it means "begot" (NAB). Goodspeed, Moffatt, and the Living Bible read "molded." But you may be quite sure that such thoughts never crossed the mind of the human poet who penned these sublime lines. My belief in the incarnation of our Lord does not tremble on the scales while scholars are searching for the precise translation of *ganah*. Before the hills in order stood or earth received her frame, God is Wisdom, and divine Wisdom was embodied in a man named Jesus. The point of this essay is not to delve overmuch into the deeps of technical theology, but to suggest that the Wisdom (or Word) who shaped the hills rejoices to dwell in your home.

The chapter ends as Wisdom sings:

> He who finds me finds life
>   and obtains favor from the Lord;
> but he who misses me injures himself;
>   all who hate me love death   (8:35–36).

The introductory section of Proverbs concludes with a picture of two women, Wisdom and Folly. Each has prepared a banquet. Each invites the passerby,

> "Whoever is simple, let him turn in here"
>   To him who is without sense she says ...   (9:4,16).

Wisdom invites the fool to abandon his foolishness and to live.

> For by me your days will be multiplied,
>   and years will be added to your life   (9:11).

Some excellent translations, including the Revised Standard Version, do not treat Folly as the personification of wrong living but understand the passage as the last warning in the introduction against the adventuress. I follow the scholars who believe that Folly here is personified, to symbolize the wide gate and the easy way that leads to destruction (Matt. 7:13). The Hebrew will readily admit either interpretation.

When I was a boy the only wisdom I ever discovered in Greek mythology was the story of Hercules at the crossroads, where Duty invited him to go one way and Pleasure called to another. Now in Proverbs I see much the same contrast between the call of Wisdom and the call of Folly. The path of Wisdom is strait and narrow, but, as Jesus said, it leads to life (Matt. 7:14). The house of Folly is filled with attraction; her death's head is so artfully covered with cosmetics that she seems the epitome of life and freedom and everything good that a growing boy or girl desires. Her voice is filled with allure as she calls to the passerby:

> Stolen waters are sweet,
>   and bread eaten in secret is pleasant.
> But he knoweth not that the dead are there;
>   and that her guests are in the depths of hell   (9:17–18, KJV).

4

The Women

Language is a fascinating phenomenon that reflects, more or less accurately, the world we live in. The word "man," for example, means either an adult human male or the entire human race. "The brotherhood of man" used to be a beloved phrase charged with deep meaning. It meant that the king is "brother" to the swineherd. It also meant that the queen is "brother" to the scullery maid. Until the recent past, the logical absurdity did not trouble anyone. Those of us (male and female) who cared about the matter had our hands full getting people on different social levels to talk with one another.

I speak as a participant in the battle for women's freedom, not as a spectator, when I report that only in recent years have I heard loud objection to sexist language. I wish those who object would provide the rest of us with workable substitutes, rather than railing at us when we use words to mean what they have meant for the past five centuries. How would you express concisely the spiritual kinship between the queen and the scullery maid? The sisterhood of squaw? When I contemplate "chairperson" my level of expectation is not high.

The language of Proverbs has a masculine slant, particularly in translation. The Hebrew word *adam* has the same double-barreled meanings that "man" has in English. When a personal

44

noun follows, the translators have to say "man" and "he"; what else could they say without getting into a monstrosity? For example:

> Good sense makes a man (*adam*) slow to anger,
> and it is his glory to overlook an offense   (19:11).

A Hebrew girl, learning this proverb, would not think that it was aimed exclusively at her brother. The Hebrew is *adam* in just about half the proverbs where the English reads "man"; in the other half, the word is *ish,* which means an adult human male (and on occasion: each, everyone, someone, anyone, or the impersonal "one"). So I suggest that the English-speaking reader of Proverbs ignore the apparent gender of any particular passage and concentrate on what it says. If the shoe fits, put it on.

I have pointed out that the first of the wise mentioned in the Bible was a woman whose extraordinary courage and dramatic talent changed the course of history (II Sam. 14:1–20). I have pointed out that the mother of Lemuel was among the human agents through whom the Holy Spirit brought Proverbs to us (31:1–9). I have suggested that many other proverbs may have been composed by women, though I will not be in a position to prove it until we meet in heaven.

Women in the Old Testament were not the shriveled caricatures envisioned by contemporary non-thought. Miriam, for example, was a prophetess, a dynamo with all the drive, intellectual power, and respect of the people accorded to her brothers, Moses and Aaron (Exod., *passim*). Another prophetess, Deborah, was among the first judges after the Hebrew conquest of the Holy Land. In addition to her spiritual and governmental gifts, she was a skilled military strategist (Judg. 4–5). When King Josiah learned of the need to reform spiritual practices, he sent his advisers to inquire of the Lord; they turned to the prophetess Huldah, though they had an abundance of her male colleagues whom they could have consulted (II Kings 22:1–20). Women in the Old Testament were not all shy violets, they were individuals, some strong, some weak, some straightforward, some devious. In qualities of personality they closely resembled the men of the Old Testament, and us.

Social conditions in ancient time differed greatly from those of today. Most of us would be acutely uncomfortable with practices that our forebears took for granted; I strongly suspect they would be horrified at a good many conditions we consider commonplace. In reading Proverbs, or any other part of the Bible, draw a distinction between the Word of God, which is unchanging, and social customs, which change daily. Since the Bible is rooted in history, it must depict social customs as they existed at the time of the events described. I do not wish a return to ancient customs; we can read better by electric light than we could by an oil lamp. I urge you to seek, and apply, the unchanging Word of God in a book that was written a long time ago.

A hypersensitive woman, upon learning that I was interested in Proverbs, stormed that it is an anti-feminist tract. She cited four proverbs, quoted in another chapter, which indicate that the world might be a nicer place if some women improved their manners (e.g., 19:13). She mentioned the frequent references to the harlot and the adventuress (e.g., 23:27), and that Folly is personified as a woman (9:13–18). She put her finger squarely upon a difficulty male preachers face every Sunday. We have only two genders to choose from, and if we hint that women are sometimes sinners, some of them get irritated with us. (Thereby demonstrating that we are right?)

Try the opposite approach. Wisdom is personified as a woman (1:20–33; 8:1–36; 9:1–12; 14:1). It takes two to commit adultery, one of whom must be male. For every proverb where a woman is in the wrong, about ten show a man in the wrong; three successive verses, each using *ish*, speak of "a worthless man," "a perverse man," and "a man of violence" (16:27, 28, 29). I am far from advocating that men avoid Proverbs because of its obvious feminist bias; I suggest that the difference between men and women is physical, not spiritual, and that a person of either gender can, with profit, take the teachings of Proverbs to heart. A woman of violence, for example, is no prize.

My irritated higher-critic of the Bible likewise snorted that in Proverbs a woman had the sole choice between being a farmer's wife and being a harlot. I could have pointed out, but 15:1 dissuaded me, that a girl had twice as many choices as a boy had in those days. A boy had a choice between being a farmer. Before the industrial revolution it took about nine people on the farm to support one person in town. Tantalizing careers in the arts, in business, in finance, or the sciences did not beckon to the growing girl. They didn't beckon to her brother, either. This does not mean that life was necessarily dull and stultifying, nor does the present variety of choice mean that life is necessarily rich and fulfilling.

One enigmatic proverb may even exalt women above men, rather than placing all of God's children on a par:

> A charming woman wins respect;
>   high-handed men win only wealth   (11:16, Moffatt).

Dr. Moffatt believed, as I do, that "only" is implied by the thrust of the verse, though the Hebrew does not demand it. Certainly Proverbs exalts spiritual wealth above fiscal prosperity, and Proverbs constantly urges men, and women, to live so that others will respect them. In the twentieth century I know and highly respect quite a few gracious women, and I have seen quite a few men sell their souls for money. (I know gracious men and miserly women, too.) If indeed this verse is a contrast between the virtues of women and those of men, to the disparagement of the latter, it is the only such contrast in the entire book. The rest show man and woman in strong partnership (with occasional moments of irritation to be sure), toiling together, bearing the mystery of life together, carrying the burdens of the family together, sharing the infinitely hard work of discipline, and together reaping the glad harvest of love from their children. Proverbs does not depict master and slave, but husband and wife.

One of the most beautiful poems ever written is found in the concluding chapter of Proverbs where the Word of God sings the praise of the courageous woman.

> Who can find a virtuous woman?
>   for her price is far above rubies.
> The heart of her husband doth safely trust in her,
>   so that he shall have no need of spoil.
> She will do him good and not evil
>   all the days of her life.

She seeketh wool, and flax,
   and worketh willingly with her hands.
She is like the merchants' ships;
   she bringeth her food from afar.
She riseth also while it is yet night,
   and giveth meat to her household,
   and a portion to her maidens.
She considereth a field, and buyeth it:
   with the fruit of her hands she planteth a vineyard.
She girdeth her loins with strength,
   and strengtheneth her arms.
She perceiveth that her merchandise is good:
   her candle goeth not out by night.
She layeth her hands to the spindle,
   and her hands hold the distaff.
She stretcheth out her hand to the poor;
   yea, she reacheth forth her hands to the needy.
She is not afraid of the snow for her household:
   for all her household are clothed with scarlet.
She maketh herself coverings of tapestry;
   her clothing is silk and purple.
Her husband is known in the gates,
   when he sitteth among the elders of the land.
She maketh fine linen, and selleth it;
   and delivereth girdles unto the merchants.
Strength and honour are her clothing;
   and she shall rejoice in time to come.
She openeth her mouth with wisdom;
   and in her tongue is the law of kindness.
She looketh well to the ways of her household,
   and eateth not the bread of idleness.
Her children arise up, and call her blessed;
   her husband also, and he praiseth her.
Many daughters have done virtuously,
   but thou excellest them all.
Favour is deceitful, and beauty is vain:
   but a woman that feareth the Lord, she shall be praised.
Give her of the fruit of her hands;
   and let her own works praise her in the gates (31:10–31,
   KJV).

A Jewish family, according to an old tradition, recites this poem on the Sabbath evening. The practice is worthy of Christian emulation. The poem raises a question in the mind of a girl: What kind of woman am I becoming? It raises questions in the mind of her brother: What kind of partner will I seek when I am a man? What kind of partner will I be? The mother and father, who know the constant temptation to deviate from the God-directed path, are reminded again of the vows they have made, each to the other and both to God.

By numerical coincidence, Job 31 gives a superb picture of the godly man. I have suggested, as pointedly as I can, that noble or base qualities are not linked to gender; a man or a woman can read and take to heart either of these two magnificent chapters. You will notice that neither chapter mentions what the person does in the house of worship. Each emphasizes living the faith in the home, in the market place, at the city gate. I mentioned that the Epistle of James in the New Testament has been called the last of the great wisdom literature. That salty letter sums up what these glorious poems say: "Show me your faith apart from your works, and I by my works will show you my faith" (James 2:18).

I am well aware that I have spoken of the "courageous" woman, while the King James Version calls her "virtuous" and the Revised Standard Version calls her "good." Looking farther afield, I find that the Jerusalem Bible reads "perfect," and the New American Bible "worthy," while the New English Bible and R. B. Y. Scott say "capable." Among the English translations, the one that comes closest to my understanding is the American Jewish Version that reads "a woman of valor." Ancient versions bear us out. In the Greek Septuagint, about the third century before Christ, she is *andreian*, courageous. In the Latin Vulgate, the fourth century after Christ, she is *fortem*, strong. For all that, "virtuous" (KJV) used to mean "courageous"; so I am going back to the intent of the King James Version.

All the above translations are valid; for Hebrew words often carry a heavy cargo of meaning. But I discovered something that startled me as I tracked the word (*chayil*) through the Old Testament. When it applies to a man, the translators always use a term to suggest aggressive courage. It is "valor" in I Samuel 10:26, for example. Frequently it means an army, a collection of brave men (e.g., Ps. 136:15). When the identical word applies to a woman, modern translators choose something meek and domesticated. Is there no need for men to be perfect, worthy, virtuous, good, and capable? Have women no need of courage?

To continue my polite disagreement with the King James Version and the Revised Standard Version, the Hebrew in the first verse does not require a question mark. The verse is stronger as an affirmation:

> When one finds a worthy wife
> her value is far beyond pearls   (31:10, NAB).

Whether expressed as a question or affirmation, the verse means that one privileged to live with a God-directed person knows riches that Wall Street cannot buy. The difference between a ruby and a pearl, to a jeweler, is enormous. To a poet, there is no difference. Each represents immeasurable wealth; the right partner in marriage is worth far more. The first mentioned, and perhaps the greatest treasure in a happy marriage, is confidence, "The heart of her husband trusts in her."

King James translates the next line literally, "He shall have no need of spoil." Contemporary versions interpret it: "He will have no lack of gain" (RSV; AJV is similar); "and never lose by that" (Moffatt); "has an unfailing prize" (NAB); "she will richly satisfy his needs" (TLB); "he is well compensated for it" (R. B. Y. Scott). I think the worst of these interpretations is, "from her he will derive no little profit" (JB). It may be true that a hard-working wife is a good investment, but that is not what the Word of God means.

There is a subtle suggestion in the word "spoil," the loot that a soldier gathered from a conquered city. This was not the soldier's wage, but a bonus that came from victory. Though the ensuing verses speak respectfully of the courageous wife's business activities, the bonus to the husband is not measurable in financial terms. Her worth is above that of any gem. You can set a price on the finest ruby or pearl in the world, but there is no way to value the richness of love in the home.

Love—the kind of love Proverbs is talking about—is not measured by the pitter-patter in the heart, but in daily action: "She will do him good and not evil all the days of her life." Most of the good pictured is economic activity. I thought long about using this poem to develop the thoughts in the chapter "The Protestant Ethic." All the classic economic virtues are here. Industry: she "worketh willingly with her hands": "her hands hold the distaff"; she "eateth not the bread of idleness." Thrift: "she perceiveth that her merchandise is good"; "she is not afraid for the snow for her household." Foresight: "she considereth a field and buyeth it"; "she bringeth her food from afar." The capitalistic virtues are indeed listed here, but this is not the chief reason for praising the courageous woman. We all know women who are superb housekeepers, whose financial affairs are always in perfect order, and who are—in other respects—a mess.

Everything significant I'll say later in the chapter on "The Perilous Blessing of Speech" has been summed up in one sentence at the end of Proverbs:

> She openeth her mouth with wisdom,
> and in her tongue is the law of kindness (31:26, KJV).

Use that sentence for a period of meditation. Consider every implication of "wisdom," "law," and "kindness." God put this message in His Word so that we would ponder it and then act on it.

The courageous woman is considerate. Caring for her own family is her primary responsibility. But likewise she cares for those who are in her employ; she gives "a portion to her maidens." Today, when household servants are rare, we tend to forget how many people work for us: the young woman at the supermarket, the young man at the drugstore, the host of people whose daily work makes our lives possible. The courageous woman cares for them, just as she cares for "her household." Further, she exemplifies a concern for the poor that runs like a thread of compassion through Proverbs:

> She stretcheth out her hand to the poor;
> yea, she reacheth forth her hands to the needy (31:20, KJV).

The Hebrew uses two words for "hand"; the latter means the palm. It suggests openhanded generosity, a trait that money-minded people eye with suspicion, but those who follow Christ practice constantly (Ps. 112:9; II Cor. 9:9).

The picture of the courageous woman is not an impossible dream. I know people who live what Proverbs is talking about. (I married one of them.) Proverbs is a book about wisdom, not wisdom for archangels, but for people like us who sweat when we are hot and shiver when we are cold, who know about fear and anxiety and temptation, who sometimes want to lay down the burden and run away. Wisdom promises that if we commit our ways to the Lord, he will direct our paths. Jesus expressed the same thing in two words, "Follow me."

Proverbs ends with a picture of one who has accepted the invitation. I said that this picture, like that in Job, does not emphasize what the godly person does in church. Worship does not end when the pastor pronounces the benediction. What we do on Tuesday and Wednesday ought to be an extension of what we do in the Lord's house on the Lord's day. Buying or selling, talking on the telephone, putting a bandage on Junior's skinned knee (and sometimes on his heart), sharpening a saw, or mopping the floor; these too, are acts of worship. I have tried to say these things, but Proverbs has said them better:

> Favor is deceitful, and beauty is vain;
>   but a woman that feareth the Lord, she shall be praised.
> Give her of the fruit of her hands;
>   and let her own works praise her in the gates (31:30–31, KJV).

5

The Elder Looks at Marriage

Agur, the son of Jakeh, said, "I am too stupid to be a man" (*adam*, 30:2). For a stupid person, he made some quite penetrating remarks. Proverbs 30 begins with Agur trembling in awe before the utter mystery of God (See Isa. 40:12–17; Job 38–41.) Then, after sage comment about practical matters of daily life, he looks with awe at another mystery:

> Three things are too wonderful for me;
>   four I do not understand:
> the way of an eagle in the sky,
>   the way of a serpent on a rock,
> the way of a ship on the high seas,
>   and the way of a man with a maiden   (30:18–19).

Kingdoms rise and fall. There are wars and rumors of war. Social patterns, language, dress, and other externals change. But the mystery of love goes on. That sex is a part of this mystery is beyond dispute, as Agur says in 30:16 and 30:20, and as modern society bellows. But sex is only part of the mystery. Through the bitter story of Tamar (II Sam. 13), for example, the Bible tells us clearly that sex without love is hell; a fact that modern society keeps trying desperately to ignore. It is interesting that the Philistines "solved" Samson's riddle, with the help of his current infatuation, by a proverbial riddle, "What is sweeter than honey? What is stronger than a lion?" (Judg. 14:18). The answer is "love." The Philistines discreetly taunted that, however strong might be their physical attraction, a woman who would betray a man obviously did not love him.

If love isn't sex, what is it? That is the heart of Agur's wonder. A comparable passage in Wisdom 5:10–11, shows that when a ship or a bird has passed by, "There is no trace to be found." If anything leaves traces, love does. Love is the great constructive force. Love builds families, congregations, hospitals, schools, business enterprises, and everything else worth building. No, the mystery that puzzles Agur is how the thing happens. How does a snake move? How does a bird fly? We know that the wind blows and that it moves ships, but how? Why? No more can you explain the love that binds this man to this woman. It is sweeter than honey, stronger than a lion, and if you will read chapter 30 carefully, you will hear Agur saying that the mystery of family love is akin to the mystery of God.

Modern society has re-introduced some age-old practices: trial marriage, open marriage, contract cohabitation, sleeping around, shacking up, and the rest, of which Agur says with distaste:

> This is the way of an adulteress:
>   she eats, and wipes her mouth,
>   and says, "I have done no wrong" (30:20).

Sex is a physical appetite; who would deny it? But sex is more than a physical appetite; it ought to be, and can be, the supreme expression of love.

Though not all who follow Christ are called to be married, marriage is a normal and beautiful expression of Christian life. Many Christians call marriage a sacrament, on a level with holy communion and baptism, in which the bodies of the man and the woman are the visible elements of God's invisible and spiritual grace. Other Christians do not use the word "sacrament" but we all agree that marriage is sacred. By His presence Jesus blessed a marriage in Cana of Galilee (John 2:1–11), and by His presence He has been blessing marriages ever since.

As practically all married people have discovered, when two people with angular personalities make their lives one, moments of friction are inevitable. The good Lord is telling us something about ourselves through the complex story of many marriages in Scripture: Abraham and Sarah, Isaac and Rebekah, Jacob and his strong arguments in favor of monogamy, David and Bathsheba, Solomon and his harem. People in biblical times were remarkably like us. They tried the age-old experiments that are being dusted off today and found some ways of life that work and others that don't. Proverbs reports extensively on both.

Even an ideal marriage endures stormy days; it just doesn't quite go on the rocks. A few, a very few, proverbs mention the storms from a strictly masculine viewpoint. I find that men today think these hilarious; women are somewhat slower to appreciate their humor.

> As a jewel of gold in a swine's snout,
>> so is a fair woman which is without discretion   (11:22, KJV).

> A foolish son is ruin to his father,
>> and a wife's quarreling a continual dripping of rain   (19:13).

> It is better to dwell in a desert land
>> than with a contentious and fretful woman   (21:19).

> It is better to dwell in a corner of the housetop
>> than with a brawling woman and in a wide
>>> house   (25:24,KJV; 21:9 is practically identical).

Marriage is a lifetime union of a man and a woman. This idea is widely derided today by those who point out that it is better to live in love, unshackled by vows, than to live in hatred because of vows that have ceased to be meaningful. If that is the alternative, one could scarcely argue. But there is another possibility: live in love that grows with the years. How can you guarantee that? In human affairs there are few guarantees, but there are statistical probabilities by which a prudent person must be guided. You can't prove that the bus marked "Chicago" will get there, but I'd suggest you take it, if that's where you want to go. Marriage like every other human enterprise, involves uncertainty and the leap of faith, as the elder suggests:

> House and wealth are inherited from fathers,
>   but a prudent wife is from the Lord   (19:14).

If certainty is not for us in this world, still we can exercise prudence. A young man, contemplating marriage, might well ask if the young woman in question gives promise of becoming the kind of woman described in Proverbs 31. A young woman might with profit look at the way a man treats his mother. The chances are excellent that he will treat his wife in much the same way. Is he considerate and helpful today? The probability is high that he will continue on that path (22:6). Is he the type of person depicted with scorn in 19:24–29? Marriage is not likely to reform him.

The best time to think about the wisdom of marriage is beforehand. Marry in haste, repent at leisure. Although the elder probably was not thinking of the vows a man and woman take to God and to each other, his words apply to marital vows as a particular application of a general rule.

> It is a snare for a man to say rashly, "It is holy,"
>   and to reflect only after making his vows   (20:25).

Practically all weddings are happy; it's living together afterward where the difficulties become acute. How does this particular couple make their home the sort that will endure? Grandma pointed out, "Cookin' lasts, kissin' don't." But good cooking, good providing in general, though important, is not a sufficient foundation for a home. Nobody can guarantee a golden wedding anniversary. But in the past ten years every golden wedding reception I have attended has been that of a couple who have tried to make their marriage an expression of their faith. They lived the proverb:

> In all your ways acknowledge him
>   and he will make straight your paths   (3:6).

Your ways are your daily activities. Acknowledge God when you buy groceries. Acknowledge God when your temper flares up. Acknowledge God when your neighbor is being unreasonable. Acknowledge God when you make love. Acknowledge God with your pocketbook. Acknowledge God when the children are being loveable and when they are somewhat less. Acknowledge God in all your ways and he will direct your path toward a golden wedding anniversary.

Perhaps the proverb reminds you of a divine command: "Make straight in the desert a highway for our God" (Isa. 40:3; Matt. 3:3). It's the same verb, "make straight" (*yashar*). A couple who try to walk each day with God will find that the eternal Creator of heaven and earth longs to be their road-builder.

Marriage is holy, natural, and blessed by God. It does not follow that everyone who falls in love ought to marry within the next twenty minutes. Proverbs, which can be celestial in one passage, can be extremely down to earth in the next; and so with the founding of a home:

> Prepare your work outside,
>   get everything ready for you in the field;
>   and after that build your house   (24:27).

The counsel, expressed in terms of a farming society, has a bitterly modern application. First make financial provision for a family, then found it. It simply is not true that two can live as cheaply as one. Living on love is a time-tested way of destroying love, and installment buying follows close behind.

Though Proverbs exalts the value of money rather more than our Christian sensibilities relish, Proverbs likewise assures us that the economic provisions for a God-centered home need not be lavish.

> Better is a dinner of herbs where love is
>   than a fatted ox and hatred with it   (15:17).

Sociological studies have demonstrated that below the break-even point, the absence of money is destructive to marriage.

Above that point additional money does not make a marriage more successful. We have material needs which no amount of piety can remove. The great American heresy is thinking that all problems can be settled by throwing money at them. The sad evidence of our divorce courts is that money, though necessary, is not the universal solvent.

In the extended introduction to Proverbs, The Glory of Wisdom, we encountered a poem in praise of married love. This poem shows the biblical delight in what God made delightful, the sexual relationship of husband and wife.

> Drink water from your own cistern,
>   flowing water from your own well.
> Should your springs be scattered abroad,
>   streams of water in the streets?
> Let them be for yourself alone,
>   and not for strangers with you.
> Let your fountain be blessed,
>   and rejoice in the wife of your youth,
>   a lovely hind, a graceful doe.
> Let her affection fill you at all times with delight,
>   be infatuated always with her love   (5:15–19).

The Song of Songs calls the beloved wife "a garden fountain, a well of living water, and flowing streams from Lebanon" (Song 4:15). Following the admonition that the married couple should love each other is a sharp question and then a sharp statement that physical love should not be shared with "strangers." The Revised Standard Version, with the contemporary Christian confusion of prudery with modesty, paraphrases a line, "Let her affection fill you at all times with delight." R. B. Y. Scott translates literally, and beautifully, "May her breasts always intoxicate you! May you ever find rapture in loving her!" Dr. Scott likewise suggests that 6:22 be appended to this poem. As translated in the Revised Standard Version, 6:22 refers to the "commandment" and the "teaching" in 6:20. The footnote says, somewhat inaccurately, that the Hebrew reads "it." Hebrew has only the masculine and the feminine genders so "it" is frequently the only legitimate translation; in this case the text reads "she." As Dr. Scott translates the verse it forms a beautiful conclusion to a superb poem.

Whatever you do, she will help you;
  When you lie down to rest she will cherish you,
When you awake she will talk with you   (6:22, R.B.Y. Scott).

Many marriages fail because husband and wife talk *at* not *with*, each other.

Even before all that unpleasantness in the Garden of Eden the Lord said to our early ancestors, "Be fruitful and multiply" (Gen. 1:28). In Old Testament thought, children were considered God's richest blessing (e.g., Ps. 127:5); barrenness was a tragedy (e.g., Gen. 11:30). It is only within the recent past, and chiefly as a consequence of our learning to control childhood diseases, that human productivity has seriously threatened our planet's capacity to produce food. One can scarcely blame the wise in biblical time for failing to solve a problem that we, with all our accumulated knowledge and computers, have not solved. However, the wise insisted constantly upon the practical, upon responsibility for one's actions, upon moderation, upon counting the cost, and upon using one's intelligence to the utmost. I believe that a wise elder from ancient time, if he could be transplanted to modern society, would be a strong advocate of family planning. Ideally, this means that every child is wanted, by parents who can fulfill their responsibilities.

The biblical elders would be bewildered by the contemporary accent on youth; perhaps that is one reason why we call them wise. I have seen families where the child was the master of the house. I have seen a twelve-year-old boy order his mother about like a flunky. I have heard an eleven-year-old girl tell her father, "Shut up." I have heard parents wail about their seven-year-old children, "Of course we know they shouldn't act this way, but what can we do?" Agur has a bit to say to such children, with somewhat less than his usual tact:

The eye that mocks a father
  and scorns to obey a mother
will be picked out by the ravens of the valley
  and eaten by the vultures   (30:17).

A young woman said to her grandmother, "The baby's a year old; I'm going to start teaching him to obey." The grandmother said, "Dear, you're starting one year too late." I think Agur and the mother of Lemuel would have welcomed grandmother as a sister wise person. The word "obey" occurs only once in the Revised Standard Version translation of Proverbs (in the verse quoted above), yet the idea fills its lucid pages. Parents are supposed to know more than their children; they are expected to govern their household; they are God's chosen agents of *musar*.

> My son, keep your father's commandment,
>   and forsake not your mother's teaching   (6:20).

> The commandment is a lamp and the teaching a light,
>   and the reproofs of discipline are the way of life   (6:23).

Musar is derived from a root meaning "to correct." The correction may be by words, though it can refer to stronger means. That was the verb in Rehoboam's scurrilous speech (I Kings 12:14), which adds little glory to the memory of Solomon's wisdom. *Musar* is the correction of children by their parents (4:1), of nations by their rulers (Job 12:18), and of people by the Lord (3:11). So *musar* has a derived meaning of instruction, doctrine (6:23). This word, which occurs twenty times in all the rest of the Old Testament, is found thirty times in Proverbs, where it is translated, depending on context, "correction, chastening, instruction, and discipline."

Yes, the elder actually indicates three times (13:24; 23:13–14; 29:15) that spanking might not be amiss.

> Do not withhold discipline from a child;
>   if you beat him with a rod, he will not die   (23:13).

> He who spares the rod hates his son,
>   but he who loves him is diligent to discipline him   (13:24).

I hear long arguments against spanking; most of them boil down to the obvious: there is no place for brutality in dealing with a child.

One of the wisest people I ever knew taught the demonstration class in kindergarten education at a great university. In a conversation about discipline my wise friend said all the proper things; resorting to force means that a child has out-smarted the adult, and the rest. Finally I asked, "Have you ever, under any circumstances, felt it necessary to spank a child?" She answered with simple dignity, "I have." Well, that's about what the biblically wise people are saying. To hear some people talk, you would gather that children in ancient times were a welter of bruises. A few verses in Proverbs indicate that, on occasion, spanking might not be a bad idea. The *musar* of parents is the discipline of love. I have known parents who spiritually battered their children to relieve parental self-hatred; I have known parents who paddled their children in love.

A "rod" can be as thick as a two-by-four or it can be a mere twig; my mother used a hairbrush. Although I did not applaud the practice at the time, I see now that she didn't enjoy it either. She was attempting to inculcate *musar* in me. I acquired no physical or spiritual harm from her discipline. I bear deep spiritual scars from misguided attempts (I do not refer to my parents) to discipline me by verbal lashings. The third mention of "rod" in connection with a child adds a bit of psychology that modern society keeps loudly denying with the lips while loudly affirming by the results of permissiveness:

> The rod and reproof give wisdom,
> but a child left to himself brings shame to his mother   (29:15).

I can introduce you to five of the loveliest women I know, each of whom has assured me that during her childhood parental *musar* was exercised frequently by means of the acidulous proverbs quoted earlier in this chapter. These can be used like a lash; they likewise can be used with a twinkle. A child knows the difference. Nothing will ever take the place of love in child-rearing.

When a child is young, you put him in a playpen. You do this, not because you are angry with the child but because you love him. To be sure, he wants to get out so that he can fall down the steps and play in the poison ivy and be chewed on by the neighbor's dog. Since you know more about the hazards than the baby, you put him in a playpen. That is *musar* for the very young. As the child grows you enlarge the boundaries. The time comes when the child must assume full responsibility; parents no longer set the bounds. Pray God, by that time you have helped him develop his own code of *musar*, self-discipline, that will sustain him through life. An ancient military maxim states, "He who would command must first learn to obey." It works in family life too.

The heart of the counsel to parents is concisely expressed:

Train up a child in the way he should go,
   and when he is old he will not depart from it   (22:6).

By precept, by example, and by *musar* parents are to train their child in the way of wisdom. The content of this training? First, and most important, the fear of the Lord (e.g., 1:7). Then, the right and the wrong use of speech (e.g., 16:23–24). Proverbs lays a heavy emphasis upon the old-fashioned virtues of industry and thrift, both positively and negatively (12:11, 24; 20:4). Sobriety is important (20:1), as is compassion for the weak (22:22) and good manners (23:1–3). I could continue the list almost indefinitely, but my hope in writing this essay is that you will fall in love with Proverbs, take it into your hand, into your mind, into your heart, and to your family. A few portions have no visible relevance to your family life; most of the book deals with matters that confront you every day.

Proverbs does not cover all the questions that arise. It says nothing about the importance of vitamin C, nor have I discovered in its pages one single word about the necessity of toothbrushing. As Isaiah mentioned, studying Proverbs or anything else in a wooden manner is contraproductive (Isa. 28:13). No book, no ecclesiastical practice, no mechanical appliance, no gimmick of any kind whatsoever can take the place of wisdom, which in Proverbs means applying your unchanging faith to the constantly changing issues of daily life, using all the information you can gather with all the intelligence God has entrusted to you. Proverbs does not supply you with a neat answer to every question; instead, the book encourages you to develop to the utmost your endowment of gumption. Nowhere in human experience is this quality more needed than in the raising of children.

The burdens of being a parent are great; the rewards can be

immeasurable. The elder sings again and again of the joys that come when a child learns the way he should go and follows it:

> The father of the righteous will greatly rejoice;
>   he who begets a wise son will be glad in him.
> Let your father and mother be glad,
>   let her who bore you rejoice   (23:24–25).

(The negation of the same thought comes frequently: e.g., 15:20; 17:25; 19:26; 20:20.) A child comes into the world totally helpless. He cannot survive more than a few hours without attention. A miracle evolves. The properly trained child grows in stature and in favor with God and man (Luke 2:52). In turn the child becomes an adult who goes through the joyous agonies of love and marriage and parenthood.

A long time before I discovered that grandchildren are the Lord's greatest invention to date, a wise person wrote:

> Grandchildren are the crown of the aged,
>   and the glory of sons is their fathers   (17:6).

Photography has made the love of grandparents for their grandchildren an almost unbearable burden for the neighbors. We laugh at grandparental excesses, but recognize that theirs is a precious love. Now notice the conclusion of the proverb; love flows both ways. A child rejoices to boast of his forebears, if he has cause to. Is there a more urgent reason to guide your life by wisdom than the love of your children and grandchildren for you? Yes, one reason is even more urgent: your Father loves you.

6

The Perilous Blessing of Speech

Insofar as the Book of Proverbs has a format, it consists of lectures by an elder, sitting in the city gate and admonishing his students:

> Hear, O sons, a father's instruction,
>   and be attentive, that you may gain insight;
> for I give you good precepts;
>   do not forsake my teaching   (4:1–2).

I have suggested that "my son" was a convention; the elder was not necessarily akin to his students. The whole weight of the convention is to inculcate respect for the parents, in large part by encouraging them to be the kind of people who deserve respect. The elder taught with the expectation that his students would guide their lives by insight, good precepts, and teaching, which, we have seen, was the Torah, or divine law. Only a stupid person would teach young people to chant words without examining their meaning, and (most of) the elders in biblical times were not stupid.

A proverb is the summary of experience. A good teacher would help the students to apply the experience of the past to the questions of the present. Juvenile students would have juvenile understanding of the questions and the answers. Naturally, the teacher would use words as the principal vehicle of teaching—what else? But learning words was not, and never should be, the goal of teaching.

> My son, keep my words
>   and treasure up my commandments with you;
> keep my commandments and live   (7:1–2a).

By no means do I disparage the old-fashioned practice of memorizing, nor do I suggest that young people should memorize only what they are capable of comprehending at the moment. When I was a rebellious high school student, an old-fashioned teacher required me to learn some passages from Shakespeare. Just to get even with him, I likewise memorized some twaddle that, at the time, I thought was far more meaningful. Unfortunately I can still remember the twaddle—most of it—but happily some of Shakespeare's exquisite verse has remained in my mind. "When I was a child, I spake as a child, I understood as a child, I thought as a child" (I Cor. 13:11, KJV), and when I became a man I acquired a more mature perspective on what I memorized in those turbulent days.

A few years after two intermittently attentive adolescents had learned the words of some proverbs, with adolescent understanding, a young couple established what they hoped would become a God-centered home; not long after, they would be saying to their child:

> Hear, my son, and be wise,
>   and direct your mind in the way   (23:19).

The proverbs were never intended for an inner group of the wise; they were designed for the complex business of daily family life. The phrase "my son," (which means on occasion "my daughter"), was a teaching convention at one stage, and a glorious reality at another. The family is the most important place in the world to practice what Proverbs is all about (3:6), and a great deal of the success or failure of family life depends on the quality of the words spoken in the home, as Proverbs often says.

Of the 915 verses in Proverbs, 222 deal with God's dangerous gift of speech. (See James 1:26; 3:1–12.) Thus 24.26229 percent, or approximately one-fourth of an important part of the divine Word to us concerns our daily use of words. Following close after is the number of proverbs dealing with what we now call economics. If you will read the Gospels analytically, you will find that Jesus' moral teaching follows that of Proverbs in emphasis upon these two important matters: First speech, then economics, then everything else. Is it coincidence that the right use of words and money builds homes while the wrong use of speech and money destroys them?

A word involves a thought in my mind, a means of communication (such as smoke signals or dit dit dah dit shortwave radio), and reception by your mind. Ideally, when I transmit you receive what I intend. In practice it doesn't always work out quite so well. Frequently we use the same word with different understandings of its meaning. Frequently I don't, or won't, hear all of what you are saying and select an important but incomplete part. Sometimes, forgive my mentioning it, you mumble.

With all their shortcomings, words remain among God's greatest gifts to the human race. Greek philosophers used the term "word" (*logos*) for the divine wisdom, and John brought this term to the very heart of the faith (John 1:1. See discussion on Proverbs 8 in chapter 3.) Marriages fail and generation gaps develop into canyons when communication breaks down. Homes are built when family members can talk with, not past, one another.

What are words for? We use them so much that we don't ask the question. We speak, often, as unconsciously as we breathe. When a friend has a stroke and can no longer talk, we begin to appreciate the miracle of speech. In Proverbs I find six overlapping emphases concerning the purpose of words: to instruct (13:18); to persuade (18:23); to communicate feeling (12:25); to express truth (12:19); to help (11:11); and perhaps most important of all, to lubricate the machinery of life (15:4). These are emphases, not rigid divisions. For example, the phrase, "Please pass the mustard, Dear," fits all six categories. It instructs one nearby about a desired course of action. It helps to persuade the nearby person to do the desired thing. It communicates a deep desire for mustard. It implies a profound truth: What's a ham sandwich without mustard? The sentence, if acted upon, will greatly help someone, namely the one who wants the mustard. And most important of all, look what happens when you leave out the two words that contribute nothing to the other five functions, and growl, "Pass the mustard."

In Proverbs we learn rapidly—if we didn't know it already— that for every good use of a word is a corresponding bad use. Words can be used to lie, to deceive, to wound, to snarl, to debauch, to seduce, and to pour emery into the gearbox. Each proverb cited in the paragraph above exposes both sides of a truth. The Word of God is likened to a two-edged sword (Heb. 4:12), our own words have similar capabilities. When used aright, words strengthen a family; when used wrong, they destroy it.

> A gentle tongue is a tree of life,
>   but perverseness in it breaks the spirit   (15:4).

A modern proverb, derived, I believe, from 10:20, holds that speech is silver but silence is golden. Many biblical proverbs make essentially the same point. Words can be instruments of God (10:11), but on many occasions it is better to be mute than to speak.

> When words are many transgression is not lacking,
>   but he who restrains his lips is prudent.
> The tongue of the righteous is choice silver;
>   the mind of the wicked is of little worth.
> The lips of the righteous feed many,
>   but fools die for lack of sense   (10:19–21).

Much can be said in favor of keeping the mouth closed to prevent the escape of ignorance therefrom, and Proverbs says it frequently:

> Wise men lay up knowledge,
>   but the babbling of a fool brings ruin near   (10:14).

He who restrains his words has knowledge,
  and he who has a cool spirit is a man of understanding.
Even a fool who keeps silent is considered wise;
  when he closes his lips he is deemed intelligent   (17:27–28).

An ancient Norse saying develops much the same idea, "No one knows that you nothing know unless you talk too much." No loving parent, unless burdened with a headache, would wish to still the incessant chatter of children, until the time comes when a child talks with great confidence about matters he knows little about. Under such circumstances the proverb (Hebrew or Norse) could be a gentle way of inculcating a principle that will have value during the child's entire lifetime.

It is bad enough when a speaker injures himself by overmuch speech, but it is immeasurably worse when he injures another. The usual vehicle of such injury is gossip. Of the many proverbs warning against the evil of repeating what one hears, my favorite is:

For lack of wood the fire goes out;
  and where there is no whisperer, quarreling ceases   (26:20).

I have said that, following the introduction, Proverbs is not a systematic book. Even so, it exalts certain virtues and deprecates certain vices consistently and, when we consider speech, the greatest of the virtues exalted is tact.

To make an apt answer is a joy to a man,
  and a word in season, how good it is!   (15:23).

"Tact" comes from the Latin verb meaning "to touch." It means knowing what to do and say in dealing with others without giving offense, particularly in difficult situations. It need scarcely be said, in Proverbs the emphasis is upon doing and saying the right thing at the right time, not just knowing about it.

A word fitly spoken
  is like apples of gold in a setting of silver   (25:11).

Just as important is knowing what not to say and do, and not saying or doing it.

He who sings songs to a heavy heart
   is like one who takes off a garment on a cold day,
   and like vinegar on a wound (25:20).

There are some translation questions concerning the verse, of
no grave spiritual import. As the footnote in the Revised Standard Version indicates, "wound" comes from the Greek translation; the Hebrew reads "lye." Pouring vinegar upon lye can be
turbulent. Perhaps the garment in question belongs to the
wearer, who puts on thin fashionable clothing that will leave
him chilled, instead of a warm garment. Perhaps the garment
belongs to another; it is his sole protection against the winter
(Deut. 24:12–13). In either case, taking off the necessary garment is the opposite of what ought to be done.

Chapter 15 is especially rich in proverbs of tact:

A soft answer turns away wrath,
   but a harsh word stirs up anger (15:1).

A gentle tongue is a tree of life,
   but perverseness in it breaks the spirit (15:4).

The lips of the wise spread knowledge;
   not so the minds of fools (15:7).

A hot-tempered man stirs up strife,
   but he who is slow to anger quiets contention (15:18).

To make an apt answer is a joy to a man.
   and a word in season, how good it is! (15:23).

The mind of the righteous ponders how to answer,
   but the mouth of the wicked pours out evil things (15:28).

Tact is a self-effacing virtue, but genuine tact is a means of
accomplishment. Two proverbs make essentially the same
point:

The wise of heart is called a man of discernment,
   and pleasant speech increases persuasiveness (16:21).

With patience a ruler may be persuaded,
   and a soft tongue will break a bone (25:15).

We all know people who illustrate in the wrong sense the bone-breaking qualities of a soft voice. With a gentle satanic smile and in well-modulated tones they can quietly demolish hope and make you feel like a total chump. The proverb, I believe, concerns the bones that need to be broken: the modern equivalent of Goliath's skull-bone, for example.

For those among us whose motives are at times earthbound, Proverbs has a very practical suggestion about the importance of tact:

He who keeps his mouth and his tongue
keeps himself out of trouble   (21:23).

The heart of tact is sensitivity to the other person. The other person; that's the trouble. Family life involves people who have their highly individual personalities, their aches and pains, their grumbles and growls, their irrational likes and dislikes, their longings and aspirations, and all the rest that goes to make up personality. Most parents have, on occasion, wished that children were little computers into whom the ancestors could feed their accumulated wisdom so that the young would face the world with adult stability. Much as we might long, it isn't going to happen. Indeed, one father of a sixteen-year-old son told me, "When I remember what I was doing at the age of sixteen, I'm scared." Children are individuals. So are wives. So are husbands. So are grandparents.

Philosophers have coined a term "the ego-centric paradox" to express our individuality. I am I. You are you. Hence communication between us is sometimes difficult. The ego-centric paradox is that I am at the center of every picture I look at and you are at the center of every picture you look at; so essentially we see different landscapes. Proverbs says it better:

The heart knows its own bitterness,
and no stranger shares its joy   (14:10).

A feeling is incommunicable. If I say I have a pain, no test yet devised by medical science can prove that I do not have a pain, though a wise doctor (or parent) can usually make a shrewd guess about malingering. Joy, likewise, is personal and private, and in truth no "stranger" can share it. The fact of biological relationship is no guarantee of success in such sharing, as parents rapidly discover when they decide to have a heart-to-heart talk with Junior.

So there's Junior sulking in the corner. Something's bugging him. But what?

> Anxiety in a man's [or a boy's] heart weighs him down,
> but a good word makes him glad   (12:25).

Yes, but we've already looked at 25:20 which warns against singing songs to a sorrowing heart.

> The tongue of the wise dispenses knowledge.
> but the mouths of fools pour out folly   (15:2).

God knows how much I want to help Junior. How do I go about it? How do I know when to speak and when to keep silent? I know people who are still bitter about what their parents said, or failed to say, fifty years ago; words, or silence, can leave lasting wounds:

> Death and life are in the power of the tongue   (18:21a).

I want to help Junior to live, how do I go about it? Proverbs is the last place in the world to look for a snap answer to that question. If I could write a book explaining in ten easy steps how to be a genuinely helpful person, somebody else would have written the book four or five thousand years ago, and we all would have it memorized. Yet Proverbs has answered the question.

> In all your ways acknowledge him,
> and he will make straight your paths   (3:6)

Proverbs warns against the vitamin pill approach to life. The proverbs themselves are guideposts on the way to wisdom, they are not substitutes for wisdom.

> Cease, my son, to hear instruction
> only to stray from the words of knowledge   (19:27).

Faith is a lifetime program, not a series of snap answers to be tugged out of the memory when a tough question comes along. Faith is the application of wisdom to the question at hand. Indeed, Proverbs warns against any unthinking reliance on proverbs:

> Like a lame man's legs, which hang useless,
>   is a proverb in the mouth of fools   (26:7).

A fool, in the biblical sense, may have an I. Q. of 160, but the kind of wisdom we are talking about is within the grasp of one whose I. Q. is half as much.

> A righteous man who walks in his integrity—
>   blessed are his sons after him   (20:7).

The daily walk with the Lord is what Proverbs is about, not just memorizing a few sentences. If the sentences help you to walk with God, that's all the satisfaction the human authors, up in heaven, want. They want you to be a righteous person who will do and say the right thing at the right time.

Two similar proverbs contain, in conjunction, a practical suggestion:

> The lips of the righteous know what is acceptable,
>   but the mouth of the wicked what is perverse   (10:32).

> The mind of the righteous ponders how to answer,
>   but the mouth of the wicked pours out evil things   (15:28).

Righteousness involves using all the brains you have. Think, then talk. That's an important part of the daily walk with the Lord.

Tact involves saying the right thing at the right time. We all know people who have a thick coating of good manners which carries them through all sorts of social occasions. God knows, I do not disparage good manners in family relationships, when I suggest that our manners are supposed to express our inward integrity.

> Like the glaze covering an earthen vessel
> are smooth lips with an evil heart (26:23).

How can I be the kind of person who knows when to speak and when to be silent? Proverbs offers an answer that has withstood the assaults of time.

> If one gives answer before he hears,
> it is his folly and shame (18:13).

A listening ear leads straight to the understanding heart. While you are walking each day with the Lord, He will help you, if you allow Him, to hear what the other person is saying. He will make you sensitive to the other person's feelings; and that's about 98 percent of what makes the difference between a home and a place to hang the hat.

> The fear of the Lord is the beginning of wisdom,
> and the knowledge of the Holy One is insight (9:10).

In all your ways acknowledge God and he will help you to understand how to deal with Junior. It's a seven-day-a-week program and it's hard work. Really, it's easier to let Junior go to the devil (29:15), but that isn't what we want. We want, by example, by *musar*, and this chapter is about words, to train Junior in the way he should go, with a prayer that when he is old he will not depart from it (22:6).

Proverbs does not dwell on the God-given helps to walking with God. In biblical time, the priests taught much about such matters; the elders emphasized the application of the faith rather than the faith itself. But a few verses are apt and relevant. One concerns God's word to us:

> Where there is no prophecy the people cast off restraint,
> but blessed is he who keeps the law (29:18).

There are several verses which emphasize the importance of our daily conversation with God:

The Lord is far from the wicked,
   but he hears the prayer of the righteous   (15:29).

There are no easy answers, in Proverbs or anywhere else. But a large part of success in Christian family living is keeping the law, worshiping God in His house on His day, using the Holy Bible and prayer in church and at home, then bringing the precepts of faith into practice within the family.

7

The Protestant Ethic

A phrase I am perfectly willing never to hear again is "the Protestant ethic," at least as long as it remains a synonym for greed and despising the poor. My objections to the term are two: the thing described is not Protestant, and it is not ethical. To be sure, I have met nominal Protestants who worship mammon. I likewise know atheists, Mohammedans, Zen Buddhists, Jews, agnostics, and animists who adore riches and scorn the poor.

In today's society, three terms are used interchangeably: "the Protestant ethic," "the Puritan ethic," and "the work ethic." The first two ought to represent Christian teaching; the latter flatly denies it. To aid you in a study of the relationship of your faith and economic theory, I recommend, *Religion and the Rise of Capitalism* by R. H. Tawney. Though the book was published more than fifty years ago, it is still relevant, and hence has been reprinted several times. Dr. Tawney examines compassionately the struggles of our forebears in applying Christian principles to business life during centuries when feudalism was giving way to free enterprise.

At a crucial point of economic change, Puritanism exploded onto the scene and helped to accelerate the change. The Puritans exalted work as a means, perhaps the chief means, of exalting God, a thought that Proverbs upholds with joyous consistency. However, a Puritan, like you and me, was a sinner; and Dr. Tawney says of him at his worst:

> Too often, contemning the external order as unspiritual, he made it, and ultimately himself, less spiritual by reason of his contempt. Those who seek God in isolation from their fellowmen, unless trebly armed for the perils of the quest, are apt to find, not God, but a devil, whose countenance bears an embarrassing resemblance to their own. The moral self-sufficiency of the Puritan nerved his will, but it corroded his sense of social solidarity. . . . He revered God as a Judge rather than loved him as a Father, and was moved less by compassion for his erring brethren than by impatient indignation at the blindness of vessels of wrath who "sinned their mercies."

During the centuries after the Puritan movement, a shift occurred; work was exalted, not so much for the glory of God as for its own sake, and thereby became the graven image before which God's children bowed. Dr. Tawney shows somberly how the "impatient indignation" of the Puritan at his worst developed into open contempt for the poor. Many of Charles Dickens's works were an attempt to revive compassion by showing the hideous realities of poverty in his day. It seems a little rough to blame Puritans, or Protestants in general, for the denial of what they stood for.

The term "Protestant" meant originally *pro + testis*, a witness for. A true Protestant witnesses for Christ by economic behavior and in all areas of life. A Protestant is guided through moral decision chiefly by the Holy Scripture. Since Proverbs has more to say about what we now call economics than any other biblical book, we can with profit seek the genuine "Protestant ethic" in its pages.

As we have noted previously, Jesus' moral teachings deal first of all with the right and wrong use of speech, then with right and wrong attitudes and actions concerning wealth, and then with everything else. Jesus must have a hard time understanding his disciples who think it improper to talk about money in church. When you read Jesus' teachings about money, and other matters, you can't help noticing the frequency of his references to Proverbs. He does not often quote Proverbs directly; rather he demonstrates familiarity with the great concepts there, and builds upon a solid foundation.

"Economics" is the Greek word for "housekeeping." The term today refers to our necessary actions in producing, distributing, and consuming the material necessities without which there could be no spiritual life as we know it. Some books on the subject leave you feeling as if economics is one thing and what you do at the supermarket is another. Yet if you buy groceries, you are an economist. The wise elders did not slab off one part of life and call it economics. They taught that God wants to be your guide when you are producing, buying, selling, and consuming, just as much as when you are hugging the children or saying your prayers.

In all your ways acknowledge him,
and he will make straight your paths (3:6).

Can a book written under one set of economic conditions say anything meaningful to us who live with very different conditions? Yes, a great deal; not about the tools of finance but about the underlying realities. Beneath the sophistication of our economic system is the basic fact: if I have something that you want, there are several ways you can acquire it. You can steal it, take it by force, or trick me out of it. These ways—all of which are mentioned in Proverbs—destroy the relationship that ought to exist between neighbors. You can likewise give me something in exchange that I want more than the thing in question. In that way our relationship is strengthened. Usually what you give is money. Sometimes we barter goods. Sometimes you offer me time and service. A successful business transaction requires that each party be satisfied, whatever the arrangements may be.

Barter, which continues today, is as old as humanity. In primitive tribal life, specialization is a fact. One person chips flints better than anybody else in the tribe, one excels in weaving baskets, one is a skillful hunter, one tans deerskin to perfection, and one sews beautifully. Through barter, the hunter receives flints, baskets, and clothing, and the others are fed.

As society grows more complex, barter becomes increasingly difficult. How many hours of cello playing would you trade for a Harris Tweed jacket, and how would you pay the weaver and the tailor who live on opposite sides of the Atlantic? Long before civilization, people supplemented barter with media of exchange: cowrie shells, wampum, dogs' teeth, and woodpecker scalps have sufficed.

Proverbs was composed before the development of money, as we understand it. Until just a few years ago, money meant coinage, usually gold, silver, or copper, minted by a recognized authority and issued as a medium of exchange. The Hebrews did not use money until after the exile. In Solomon's time merchants used metal bars or rings, stamped with weight such as a talent or a shekel. A threshing floor and a team of oxen were worth fifty shekels of silver when David made a celebrated. purchase (II Sam. 24:24). In modern society we use metal coins only for small change; larger amounts are represented by printed pieces of paper with no intrinsic value, and even these are being displaced by credit cards and automatic deduction from bank accounts. So if I refer to the teaching of the elders about money, there is a slight inaccuracy; they didn't have money yet, and we have substituted a vast system of credit for money as our grandparents understood the term.

Our tools of economic life are very different from those of biblical times, yet the people who use the tools are remarkably similar to those who sat at the city gate and listened respectfully as a wise person addressed them, "My son. . . ." About 95 percent of the wise person's teachings about what we now call economics have an immediate, practical relevance in the twentieth century.

Some of these teachings make you shudder; they were intended to. They appear to contradict everything that Christ and the prophets say about the relative importance of wealth and human decency. At least three show the advantages of bribery (17:8; 18:16; 21:14). On several occasions the contrast between rich and poor is pointed out in terms so materialistic they make us wince (10:15; 14:20; 18:23; 19:4; 19:6–7). One of the worst is:

The poor is disliked even by his neighbor,
  but the rich has many friends   (14:20).

I suggest two ideas we might apply when reading those parts
of Proverbs that trouble us: first, the wise writers were, in general, astute people; and second, they cared about morality almost as much as we do. With these thoughts in mind, reexam-
ine the proverb. It does not say these things ought to be, but
that they are true. The wise do not admonish us to adore riches,
nor do they suggest that we hate the poor; quite the opposite.

I urge you to persevere with the Proverbs for yourself and for
your family's guidance after discovering that some proverbs
therein point to sordid realities in the world about you. The
Holy Spirit uses many avenues to your heart; sometimes the
Bible shows vividly what ought not to be.

From the scorn being heaped upon the Protestant ethic today,
you would gather that lucre is always filthy and the old-
fashioned qualities of industry and thrift should be put on the
trash-heap. From Proverbs you get a very different picture. The
wisdom there has outlasted many changes in philosophy, it is
still wise.

The elders are far from advocating mammon worship, but
they indicate that money is remarkably convenient stuff to have
around.

A rich man's wealth is his strong city;
  the poverty of the poor is their ruin   (10:15).

You might include this among the cynical proverbs mentioned above, I prefer the term factual. Money is a powerful
defense—comparable to the walls of an ancient city—against
the slings and arrows of outrageous fortune. If you have deal-
ings with the poor, you know many who were crushed and
ruined by their poverty. When the church is dealing with des-
parately poor people we try, as part of proclaiming the gospel,
to help them out of their poverty (James 2:14–17).

Christians perversely misunderstand Jesus' remark: "You
cannot serve God and mammon" (Matt. 6:24). His predecessors,
the wise elders, would have applauded the statement; they said

much the same thing. The verb "serve" (douleuein) could, with propriety, be translated "worship" (See Rom. 12:11; I Thess. 1:9.) You *can't* worship both God and money. This doesn't make money evil (or good); only our attitudes toward money are good or evil. The love of money, or any other idol, is evil (I Tim. 6:10). Money is a tool, the elders teach, that a wise person respects and uses with all the skill he can to achieve the great aims of life.

The Proverbs, I warned you when this study began, is an old-fashioned book. The principles therein have been tried and rejected and brought back a thousand times because they work in our hustle-bustle society. The business of the world always has been, and always will be, conducted by people who practice industry and thrift. Proverbs has much to say in favor of the hard work that is necesssary to acquire and keep material wealth. I could quote dozens of these maxims, but three will give the general flavor:

> He who tills his land will have plenty of bread,
>   but he who follows worthless pursuits will have plenty of
>   poverty   (28:19).

> The plans of the diligent lead surely to abundance,
>   but everyone who is hasty comes only to want   (21:5).

> A slack hand causes poverty,
>   but the hand of the diligent makes rich   (10:4).

Much can be said, it has been said, in favor of hard work, planning, and sticking to it. Plenty of bread, abundance, and being rich are desirable states; whatever we say, we live this belief. There is a close connection between labor and the rewards of labor. (I trust you noticed the subtle allusion to get-rich-quick schemes.) The only people I know who despise wealth are those so rich that they have learned what money cannot buy. They do not carry their disdain to its obvious conclusion; they recognize that it will buy some things that are nice to have, groceries, for instance.

Children in the twentieth century have a tendency toward sloth, in which regard they are identical with their predecessors in biblical times. The word "sluggard" occurs nowhere else in the Bible, but fourteen times in Proverbs. Yet the idea occurs far more frequently; in the proverbs just cited the sluggard is "he who follows worthless pursuits" and "a slack hand." I indicated above that sometimes a proverb means the exact opposite of what it says. I suggest, however, that the proverbs heaping scorn upon the sin of sloth mean literally and precisely that sloth is evil.

We have considered the superb parable, The Sluggard's Vineyard (24:30–34), which is the longest extended discussion of sloth in Proverbs. In 6:8, the sluggard is admonished to follow the example of the ant who "prepares her food in summer and gathers her sustenance in harvest." When you hear a boy moaning in agony because he must carry the laundry up from the basement, a waggish proverb might occur to you:

> The sluggard buries his hand in the dish;
>   it wears him out to bring it back to his mouth   (26:15).

You might even mention the proverb to the young man in question, if the circumstance is appropriate. The proverb is remarkably similar to our perennial joke (which isn't a proverb because no one has expressed it concisely) about the man who was screaming in pain because he sat on a tack and was too lazy to get off.

My favorite proverb condemning laziness—and one of the funniest lines in the entire Bible—is:

> The sluggard says, "There is a lion outside!
>   I shall be slain in the streets!"   (22:13).

How can you, without nagging, communicate to a growing child your lack of admiration for his great skill in making excuses? You might try the good-humored approach; it has helped many other parents when they wanted to tear out their hair.

The handmaid of industry is thrift, a virtue that Proverbs extols with joyous consistency. As a pastor I have talked with hundreds of people, many of them with tears in their eyes, who bitterly regretted spending money on nonessentials when they came to a crisis that could have been averted with the money they wasted. I have yet to talk with a family who regretted having some savings when they needed them. Two pungent proverbs sum up the idea that underlies the teaching about thrift:

Know well the condition of your flocks,
  and give attention to your herds;
for riches do not last for ever;
  and does a crown endure to all generations?
When the grass is gone, and the new growth appears,
  and the herbage of the mountains is gathered,
the lambs will provide your clothing,
  and the goats the price of a field;
there will be enough goats' milk for your food,
  for the food of your household
  and maintenance for your maidens   (27:23–27).

There is precious wealth where a wise man dwells,
  but the man who is stupid consumes it   (21:20, R.B.Y. Scott).

Although the wise never heard of installment buying, some of the proverbs have a direct bearing upon the practice. As any pastoral counselor will assure you, debt can be a wonderful servant but is a cruel master.

The rich rules over the poor,
  and the borrower is the slave of the lender   (22:7).

Many proverbs about thrift are couched in a form that is obscure to the modern reader. For example:

Take a man's garment when he has given surety for a stranger,
  and hold him in pledge when he gives surety for
  foreigners   (20:16).

In some "surety" proverbs, the King James Version uses the term "strike hands" which is simply baffling today. Proverbs was composed long before banks, as we understand them, came into being. Then, as now, a person wishing to make a purchase often did not have the resources to do so. So the people of the

Near East evolved a system by which one person made himself liable for the obligations of another. In the presence of witnesses the guarantor would "strike hands" with the lender and promise to pay the debt in case the borrower defaulted. It was a necessary part of economic life, and, though the outward forms have changed, the practice continues today, as you will learn readily if you try to get a bank loan without having any collateral.

Like every other good thing, the practice of giving surety could be abused. The guarantor would be superhuman if he did not have feelings of pride that others turned to him in their necessity. Pride, then as now, often led people into making unwise guarantees (6:1–5). Proverbs does not condemn suretyship, but the book warns over and again, for God's sake, and for your family's sake, be careful. Most of the "surety" warnings mention the hazard of dealing with "strangers" or "foreigners." If you know and can reasonably trust a person, that's one thing. If you don't know him, he may or may not be trustworthy; it's best to find out before putting yourself in his power.

As an adult, quite familiar with Proverbs, I sedulously ignored the wise council of the elders. I endorsed a sixty dollar check for a person with an extremely bad credit record, but naively (in 17:18 KJV the elder graciously intimates that I was "void of understanding"), I thought that the person in question would not swindle me. Some months later a lawyer said sadly, "I suggest that you decide you've bought sixty dollars of experience." No, the sheriff didn't foreclose on me and my creditors didn't take away my bed, but it was amazing how many needs rose that month, frivolities like shoes for the children, that were postponed because I didn't pay attention to Proverbs. The elders never heard of a checking account, but I wish I had applied their advice to endorsing checks.

If Proverbs said no more about economics, it would be the guiding star for the so-called Protestant ethic. Proverbs has pointed out the value of industry and thrift, the importance of riches—so important that they can destroy what is good and decent in people. Proverbs has condemned sloth in vigorous terms. All this fits superbly with the work-ethic which is the unconscious philosophy of some people you talk with every day.

The proverbs quoted are all part of God's Word, which really ought to be read with a measure of intelligence. Sometimes God wants you to say, "No, Lord, you don't really mean that." (Eccles. 10:19, for instance.) But most of the proverbs mean literally what they say: Wealth has considerable value in this world; a wise person works hard, earns, and saves; a fool and a sluggard throw money away. Even so, the proverbs extolling wealth and the advantages thereof are few compared with those showing the dangers of ambition not guided by wisdom.

I mentioned three proverbs pointing to the fact that bribery is sometimes successful. In a world where this is the case, Proverbs says concisely:

> A wicked man accepts a bribe from the bosom
>   to pervert the ways of justice   (17:23).

You couldn't get much clearer than that. The Word of God says that although a practice may bring a visible benefit, it is wicked and it destroys justice, which is a primary goal of life for a person who seeks to be wise.

The principal use of Proverbs is in the home, to help develop the attitudes of growing children. It is not difficult for children from Christian homes to pick up snobbish attitudes; it is only too easy to laugh at those who lack fine clothes or good manners. I do not suggest that the cynical proverbs quoted above are a proper diet for the young; rather try these:

> He who despises his neighbor is a sinner,
>   but happy is he who is kind to the poor   (14:21).

> Better is a poor man who walks in his integrity
>   than a rich man who is perverse in his ways   (28:6).

Jesus, as was His custom, took up the teaching of the wise and ennobled it even further. He taught:

> Blessed are you poor, for yours is the kingdom of God.
> Blessed are you that hunger now, for you shall be satisfied.
> Blessed are you that weep now, for you shall laugh. Luke
>   6:20–21

Even so, when people were hungry Jesus fed them, and so should we.

A child who grows in a home where Christlike attitudes are taught and practiced will react vigorously to a proverb about the poor person who is despised by his neighbor. He will decide: Here's one neighbor who isn't going to dislike a poor person because he is poor and isn't going to like a rich person because he is rich.

For every proverb that mentions the disadvantages of being poor, about five urge compassion. The one just mentioned says that he who looks down on his neighbor is a "sinner." The same thought is expressed in far stronger terms:

> He who oppresses a poor man insults his Maker,
> but he who is kind to the needy honors him   (14:31).

Concern for the needy who are nearby or far away is a necessary component of the Protestant ethic. The church has obeyed Christ's commandment to go into all the world (Matt. 28:19–20), proclaiming the gospel in words and through such tools of salvation as medical care, education, and food for poor people, all of which cost money.

For every proverb that points to the value of wealth, about ten fall into a category that I call "The Boundaries to Ambition." Chief among these boundaries is old-fashioned honesty.

> Bread gained by deceit is sweet to a man,
> but afterward his mouth will be full of gravel   (20:17).

> The getting of treasure by a lying tongue
> is a fleeting vapor and a snare of death   (21:6).

One proverb exalting honesty is often quoted and almost as often cheapened by misunderstanding.

> A false balance is an abomination to the Lord,
> but a just weight is his delight   (11:1; see also 16:11; 20:10;
> 20:23).

I have known people to shrug this off as another version of our proverb, "Honesty is the best policy." Policy is what benefits, or seems to benefit, you. That is not what the proverb exalts. Instead, the divine Word lifts chaffering in the marketplace up to the presence of God. Each proverb cited recognizes the obvious, that some merchants seek a thievish advantage, using one set of weights to buy and another when they sell. Each of the four tells the one who loves God to demonstrate that love, not only in singing hymns but in buying or selling onions.

Throughout the Book of Proverbs we find a frank recognition that the things God made are good, when acquired honestly and used wisely. This is not materialism, a philosophy that makes a god of things. You appreciate a coat to keep you warm, a roof to keep you dry, a book to read, and a steady light to read by. These are good things. You work hard to earn the money to buy them. Your work and your spending are stewardship of the energies and opportunities God has entrusted to you. Getting and spending are not the goals of your life, though. They are part of what you do in pursuit of something better.

My concordance shows twenty proverbs saying that something is "better" than something else that is desirable. Six of them say that wisdom is better than wealth (e.g., 16:16). Proverbs 16:8 says that righteous poverty is better than great revenue with injustice. Verse 19 of that same chapter says that a humble spirit is better than the pride of the wealthy. Proverbs 19:22 honors a poor man as better than a liar and 22:1 urges that a good name is better than great riches. Proverbs 28:6 says that integrity is better than wealth.

Two proverbs were placed with loving care, one after another.

> Better is a little with the fear of the Lord
>   than great treasure and trouble with it.
> Better is a dinner of herbs where love is
>   than a fatted ox and hatred with it   (15:16–17).

Do you notice the exquisite parallelism? Three parallels are what we called in the first chapter "synonymous parallelism." A little is, in culinary terms, a dinner of herbs. A fatted ox is one form of a great treasure. Trouble and hatred are not far apart. It's the other parallel that I point to. In chapter 1 we called it "constructive parallelism": where fear of the Lord is genuine, family love flourishes. Poor people, who sit around a table however crude, and eat their simple meal with love for God and each other, are the richest people in the world.

Agur, who says many cogent things in one short chapter, sums up the economic philosophy underlying Proverbs in one sentence that could serve as a guide for every Christian family.

> Remove far from me falsehood and lying;
>> give me neither poverty nor riches;
>> feed me with the food that is needful for me,
> lest I be full, and deny thee,
>> and say, "Who is the Lord?"
> or lest I be poor, and steal,
>> and profane the name of my God   (30:8–9).

8

Your Faith and Your Neighbor

A family lives in a neighborhood, scattered or compact. The relationship of family members with the neighbors has a deep effect upon their relationships with one another. Not surprisingly, Proverbs has much to say about the subject. The heart of the instruction is to seek the company of those who aspire to wisdom and to be the kind of person whose company wise people will enjoy.

Your interaction with others helps to decide—for good or for ill—what kind of person you are.

Iron sharpens iron,
and one man sharpens another   (27:17).

The medieval rabbis understood this verse to mean that biblical studies are best conducted in the company of other students. In this way different opinions are sharpened against one another, and from the conflict of ideas truth emerges. Without denying this, we may give the thought a wider application. Our contact with others helps to form our characters. Just as iron is honed to a keen edge against iron, you are shaped largely by your relationship with others—family, friends, and yes, enemies. You help to shape the lives of those who come in contact with you.

In the Revised Standard Version concordance, I find the word "neighbor" more often in Proverbs than in any other book, with the prophecy of Jeremiah following close after, and Deuteronomy close after that. The latter books share with Proverbs the emphasis on the dedicated heart rather than the externals of religious practice.

The English word "neighbor" meant originally the farmer (*bauer*) who is nigh. The principal Old Testament word, *re'eh*, has perhaps, a little more depth of meaning. "Neighbor" and "shepherd" (Ps. 23:1) are closely related; both are derived from a verb meaning to pasture a flock. Feeding is both literal and figurative; for example, "The mouths of fools feed on folly" (15:14). You could convey the meaning just as accurately by saying, "The mouths of fools delight in folly." So, by natural extension the word expressing delight came to mean a person in whose company you delight; frequently it is translated "friend." The elders were keenly aware that evil people delight in evil companionship (13:20; 28:7; 29:3). They urge you to be the loyal, compassionate person whose companionship will help others to be strong.

A friend [neighbor] loves at all times,
and a brother is born for adversity   (17:17).

"Brother" has, I believe, both the literal and the extended meaning. When your neighbor is in trouble, that's the time he most needs you as his "brother."

Proverbs is the textbook of the daily walk with God (3:6). Whether or not you walk with the Lord depends, in considerable measure, upon your human companionship on the way.

He who walks with wise men becomes wise,
but the companion of fools will suffer harm   (13:20).

The English proverb puts it, "Birds of a feather flock together." A medieval rabbi expressed much the same thought, "Would you know all about a man? Ask who his companion is."

The divergent paths suggested above are described brilliantly in 4:14–19. The way of the wicked is pictured vividly, with a penetrating observation, "They are robbed of sleep unless they have made someone stumble." I suggest a few proverbs—far from an exhaustive list—warning against those whose companionship will provide a multitude of stumbling blocks. Shun the person who speaks evil (11:9) and the talebearer (11:13). Companionship with the "wrathful man" will turn into a "snare" (22:24–25). Don't associate too closely with a stingy person (23:6–8), and be quiet in the presence of a fool (23:9). The winebibber's company does not profit (23:20–21). The seductive joys of the harlot and the adventuress bring grief (e.g., 23:27). The liar is dangerous to those about him (14:25). Scoffers are a menace; we usually overlook them in our catalogue of sinners, but Proverbs says that perpetual throwers of cold water can "set a city aflame" (29:8). A thief, obviously, is no fit companion (29:24). Many about you follow a trail that leads away from God.

The alternate path is the walk with the righteous; this you and your family are constantly urged to follow. It is pictured with one of the most beautiful verses in the Bible.

> The path of the righteous is like the light of dawn,
>   which shines brighter and brighter until full day   (4:18).

Is not this the path to which Jesus refers when He says, "I am the way" (John 14:6)? Daily association with friends who are walking with Christ helps us to walk with Him. (See also 2:20–22.)

High among the qualities to be sought in a friend, or developed in yourself, is sincerity. We all know hearty backslappers with a smile like a toothpaste advertisement whose friendship is worth, perhaps, a wooden nickel. The species was known in biblical time, and several proverbs warn against accepting such a person as friend, or being such a person.

> There are friends who pretend to be friends,
>   but there is a friend who sticks closer than a brother   (18:24).

> Trust in a faithless man in time of trouble
>   is like a bad tooth or a foot that slips   (25:19).

> A man who flatters his neighbor
>   spreads a net for his feet   (29:5; see also 26:28).

There is a delightful ambiguity about the verse. A net for whose feet, those of the flatterer or the flattered? I believe the elders would be highly amused if they could hear biblical scholars debating the issue today. The framers of the proverb quite intentionally left it ambiguous. If you fall for flattery, you are in trouble. If you flatter others, you will be in trouble sooner or later.

My favorite passage concerning the insincere neighbor is among the comparatively rare extended proverbs. Three compact verses are tied together in constructive parallelism. Notice the repeated contrast between the lips and the heart. Notice how the figure of glaze is repeated, with subtle variation, in each verse. Notice and beware of listening to (or being) such a person.

> Like the glaze covering an earthen vessel
>   are smooth lips with an evil heart.
> He who hates dissembles with his lips
>   and harbors deceit in his heart;
> when he speaks graciously, believe him not,
>   for there are seven abominations in his heart;
> though his hatred be covered with guile,
>   his wickedness will be exposed in the assembly   (26:23–26).

We have examined some proverbs warning against contempt for the poor. As we well know, there are reasons other than poverty why unneighborly people despise others, and the elders teach us to admire none of these reasons.

> He who belittles his neighbor lacks sense,
>   but a man of understanding remains silent   (11:12).

Among the sayings of Agur are four proverbs in sequence, each beginning "There are those. . . ." The first concerns disrespect for one's parents (30:11). The last depicts savagely those who exploit the poor (30:14). The third is, I think, hilarious. It leads one to suspect that the term "highbrow" has been in circulation for a long, long time.

> There are those—how lofty are their eyes,
>   how high their eyelids lift!   (30:13).

91

The second in the series ties them all together.

> There are those who are pure in their own eyes
> > but are not cleansed of their filth   (30:12).

Jesus almost certainly had this proverb in mind when he spoke so scathingly about the sins of religious people (e.g., Matt. 23:23–24). Christians consistently misunderstand our Savior on this score. He isn't warning us against dead Pharisees and Sadducees, he's urging us to look in a mirror.

It's possible to look down on your neighbor. It is likewise possible, and dangerous, to look up to the wrong neighbor.

> Fret not yourself because of evil-doers
> > and be not envious of the wicked,
> for the evil man has no future,
> > the lamp of the wicked will be put out   (24:19–20; 24:1–2 is
> > similar).

The beloved Psalm 37 develops the thought. Another proverb, even more glorious, gives a positive reason for reining in the ever-present temptation to envy.

> Let not your heart envy sinners,
> > but continue in the fear of the Lord all day.
> Surely there is a future,
> > and your hope will not be cut off   (23:17–18; 3:31–35 is
> > similar).

This is not the place to examine the complex question about the Old Testament's teaching concerning eternal life. In Jesus' time the Sadducees said, correctly, that their Bible did not explicitly teach the resurrection of the dead. The Pharisees said, correctly, that eternal life is implied in all our belief about divine justice and divine love. We are not bound to the ancient times; we can read what was written before Christ from a Christian perspective. When we see that the wicked are frequently prosperous and that the righteous often must wear a crown of thorns, we can recognize that there is a future. Psalm 73 is a brief and powerful sermon developing the idea in this verse. There you will find every temptation to envy the wicked that you have ever known. There, too, you will find the radiant faith that shines through the proverb.

Neighbors are human, hence prone to disagreement which is normal and healthy, until people get disagreeable about it. The fool is the special target of Proverbs, the sluggard next, and not far after is the quarrelsome person—male or female.

As charcoal to hot embers and wood to fire,
   so is a quarrelsome man for kindling strife (26:21).

A continual dripping on a rainy day
   and a contentious woman are alike;
To restrain her is to restrain the wind
   or to grasp oil in his right hand (27:15–16).

The difference between quarreling and contention, as I understand the terms, is chiefly a matter of volume. One yells, the other whines, and each is an abomination. To date I have discovered no link between gender and either of these characteristics; I know some men and some women who are experts at one or the other; and Proverbs sagely counsels:

Make no friendship with a man given to anger,
   nor go with a wrathful man,
lest you learn his ways
   and entangle yourself in a snare (22:24–25).

Christians are admonished, "If possible, so far as it depends upon you, live peaceably with all" (Rom. 12:18). Paul recognized, as we do, that sometimes a Christian must stand up and fight. But he echoed a thought from Proverbs: If you can honorably avoid a fight, do so.

Do not contend with a man for no reason,
   when he has done you no harm (3:30).

It is an honor for a man to keep aloof from strife;
   but every fool will be quarreling (20:3).

He who meddles in a quarrel not his own
   is like one who takes a passing dog by the ears (26:17).

The beginning of strife is like letting out water;
   so quit before the quarrel breaks out (17:14).

Picture a reservoir storing up precious water to irrigate gardens (Eccles. 2:6). A small leak in the retaining dike allows a few drops to trickle out. But each drop carries with it a grain or two of clay. So the trickle turns into a rill and the rill turns into a torrent until the dike is breached and the precious water lost.

In a numerical listing of "things which the Lord hates" we find wayward eyes, tongue, hands, heart, and feet, and then the total personality:

> . . . a false witness who breathes out lies,
>   and a man who sows discord among brothers   (6:19).

As so often happens when we read in Proverbs, we decide smugly that we are not included. We strive to speak the truth—much of the time—and we would never think of sowing discord. Would we? Well, no. But I just heard some remarkably juicy gossip, and if you'll promise not to tell. . . .

The practice of gossip begins, or ends, quite early in one's career. A loving parent who discovers that a child has tendencies toward being a tattle-tale might profitably quote a sage maxim mentioned in an earlier chapter:

> For lack of wood the fire goes out;
>   and where there is no whisperer, quarreling ceases   (26:20).

Two proverbs about gossip provide a fascinating contrast. The first line of each is practically the same, in Hebrew as in English. It's the second where the difference lies.

> He who goes about gossiping reveals secrets,
>   therefore do not associate with one who speaks
>   foolishly   (20:19).

> He who goes about as a talebearer reveals secrets,
>   but he who is trustworthy in spirit keeps a thing
>   hidden   (11:13).

Each warns against associating with a gossip. The first suggests a practical reason: if he blabs to you, he will blab about you to others. This precept is one of my guides in life. If you say that it appeals to my enlightened self-interests, I won't deny it, but

I shall continue to be guided by this precept. The other begins in the same place—the Hebrew is even closer than the English —and then upholds the goal that I want to reach, the goal that I pray my children and grandchildren will reach. To be "trustworthy in spirit"; that's what Christian life is all about. Christ went to the cross to make me a trustworthy person, whom my family, my neighbor, and my God can trust.

Several more proverbs concerning you and your neighbor fit into no neat category. Your neighborhood would be a happier place if you and your neighbors applied them.

> Remove not the ancient landmark
> which your fathers have set   (22:28; see 23:10–11).

I recall one ancient landmark with which experts are constantly tampering. It begins, "We hold these truths to be self-evident...."

> Let your foot be seldom in your neighbor's house,
> lest he become weary of you and hate you   (25:17).

The principle applies to the telephone, likewise.

> Like a madman who throws firebrands,
> arrows and death,
> is the man who deceives his neighbor
> and says, "I am only joking!"   (26:18–19).

The practical joke evidently has an ancient, if not honorable, lineage. Those who perpetrate practical jokes usually think they are screamingly funny. The victims usually scream, though not with laughter.

> Let another praise you, and not your own mouth,
> a stranger, and not your own lips   (27:2).

This proverb has been a favorite of mine for years. I have often quoted it, I hope with a smile, when young people spoke of themselves more highly than they ought to speak. Evidently somebody listened. Just a few days ago one of these young people, now a husband and father, heard a remark of mine, smiled sweetly, and repeated the proverb.

> He who blesses his neighbor with a loud voice,
>   rising early in the morning,
>   will be counted as cursing   (27:14).

A distinguished scholar named Cheyne said of this verse: "A humorous picture. Such ostentatious and inopportune salutations are execrable flattery." A friendly smile is priceless. A cheerful word of greeting brightens the whole day, but not when it is bellowed.

In its teaching about our relationship with neighbors, Proverbs reaches the loftiest ethical heights in the Old Testament. The word "neighbor" originally meant a person you like. But, unhappily, people we like, even members of our families, sometimes do things that we intensely dislike. What happens next? The normal, natural thing is to kick back, to get even. But this isn't the path that leads to the light.

> Do not say, "I will do to him as he has done to me;
>   I will pay the man back for what he has done"   (24:29).

I want to get even; God wants me to get ahead. If I return evil for evil, my former friend will retaliate, then I will retaliate, and so without end.

A cryptic proverb, open to many interpretations, shows what not to do.

> He loveth transgression that loveth strife;
>   and he that exalteth his gate seeketh destruction   (17:19,
>   KJV).

The first line is clear: quarreling leads to "transgression," against God, your neighbor, and against yourself. The second line is literally "he who makes his gate high." Many Jewish scholars understand the gate to mean the mouth; if so, this proverb emphasizes that the strife-lover is usually a loud-mouth. But R.B.Y. Scott translates the line, "To make one's doorway inaccessible is to invite destruction." That's the door of forgiveness. Quarreling leads to sin, slowness to forgive leads to destruction. The thought is intensified by another proverb which is stated more positively.

> He who forgives an offense seeks love,
>   but he who repeats a matter alienates a friend   (17:9).

It's hard, you and I know, and God knows it too, to forgive a serious wrong when the wrongdoer has apologized (Luke 17:3–5). We (you, I, and God) likewise know that frequently the wrongdoer does not apologize. He kicks us and he kicks us and he kicks us again. The wise elder counsels not to gloat even when this enemy is in trouble.

> Do not rejoice when your enemy falls,
>   and let not your heart be glad when he stumbles;
> lest the Lord see it, and be displeased,
>   and turn away his anger from him   (24:17–18).

The fourth line illustrates a perennial difficulty of religious writing. We must speak of heavenly matters with earthbound language. How can we express the fact of divine judgment without using language that suggests the human spirit in its less praiseworthy manifestations? This verse, with hundreds of others, uses "anger." The same thought is expressed by "vengeance" (Deut. 32:35; Ps. 94:1; Rom. 12:19; Heb. 10:30). The teaching of Proverbs is clear and sublime: leave judgment in the hands of God, who will extend to the sinner every bit of mercy that divine love can possibly extend. Don't envy your evil neighbor, don't gloat when he stumbles, leave him to God.

It is exceeding difficult to restrain our emotions about our enemies, but loftier and more difficult counsel follows.

> If your enemy is hungry, give him bread to eat;
>   if he is thirsty, give him water to drink;
> for you will heap coals of fire on his head,
>   and the Lord will reward you   (25:21–22).

Jesus took the thought and lifted it even higher (Matt. 5:43–48). Paul quoted these verses in what I consider his noblest ethical teachings (Rom. 12:19–21). To be sure, those coals of fire used to bother me. If my motive in feeding my enemy is to make him suffer, then I am piously returning evil for evil. However, I have suggested before that the writers of Proverbs were almost as smart as I am. They may very well have recognized that coals of fire can do more than singe and destroy. Fire, in biblical usage, is frequently cleansing. A sin-offering was burned on the altar; the prophets speak of divine forgiveness as a "refiner's fire" (e.g., Mal. 3:2). If my motive in doing good is to destroy my neighbor, that makes me an evil person. But suppose my motive is to refine the silver by burning the dross?

As a pastoral counselor I have asked people consumed with hatred to try literally what Jesus commands: "Pray for those who persecute you" (Matt. 5:44). Every person who has tried it has reported. First, it was the hardest work I ever did. Second, when I bent the reluctant knees and opened the reluctant lips to pray, something happened; a great load of hate began to dispel. The third result does not always take place; Jesus does not promise it. Often the former hostility dwindles and the former enemy becomes a friend. The coals of fire have refined away the dross of hatred and the silver of friendship remains.

> The fruit of the righteous is a tree of life;
>   and he that winneth souls is wise   (11:30, KJV).